Unity through Diversity

OSCAR CULLMANN

UNITY
through
DIVERSITY

*Its Foundation, and a Contribution to
the Discussion concerning the Possibilities
of Its Actualization*

Translated by M. Eugene Boring

FORTRESS PRESS   PHILADELPHIA

Translated from the German *Einheit durch Vielfalt—Grundlegung und Beitrag zur Diskussion über die Möglichkeiten ihrer Verwirklichung* copyright © 1986 J. C. B. Mohr (Paul Siebeck), Tübingen, West Germany.

ENGLISH TRANSLATION COPYRIGHT © 1988 BY FORTRESS PRESS

———————————

Library of Congress Cataloging-in-Publication Data

Cullmann, Oscar.
  Unity through diversity.

  Bibliography: p.
    1. Christian union.   I. Title.
BX8.2.C7713   1987   262 .0011   87-21263
  ISBN 0–8006–2047–X

———————————

2988G87   Printed in the United States of America   1–2047

Contents

CONTENTS

Editorial Note

THE FOLLOWING bibliographic information is added for the benefit of English-language audiences. For an overview of ecumenism as a "unity issue," see William G. Rusch, *Ecumenism: A Movement Toward Church Unity* (Philadelphia: Fortress Press, 1985). Another important assessment of the Lima document of 1982 *(BEM)* is that of John Reumann in *The Supper of the Lord: The New Testament, Ecumenical Dialogues, and Faith and Order on Eucharist* (Philadelphia: Fortress Press, 1985), 137–82. For reports on developments in the U.S.A., consult the monthly *Ecumenical Trends,* published by the Graymoor Ecumenical Institute, Garrison, N.Y. 10524. For reports on and documentation of ecumenical progress, one should regularly consult the publications of the World Council of Churches (Faith and Order Papers) and The Lutheran World Federation (LWF Publications 1977–1984), both in Geneva, Switzerland, and J. Puglisi, *A Workbook of Bibliographies of Interchurch Dialogues* (Rome: Centro pro Unione, 1978), and the continuing updates in the Bulletins of Centro pro Unione.

Prologue

IT IS REMARKABLE, but also perhaps understandable, that the production of ecumenical literature has increased in the same proportion as the complaints concerning the general decline of ecumenism— complaints that are only partially justified. It is not my intention that the present work unnecessarily increase the number of such publications. I believe, however, that it is incumbent upon me to make my considerable years of experience and reflections in the area of ecumenism available in a synthesis which has been arrived at independently of the ecumenical models recently proposed, but nonetheless fits into the subject of the present discussion.

Since the last Vatican Council (in which I participated as a guest of the Vatican and as an official observer), I have not been a member of the ecumenical commissions which have prepared joint texts, but I have followed their work closely and with interest. At the same time, I have attempted during this period to make my own conception of Christian unity more precise and to develop my fundamental understanding of ecumenicity. This is an understanding that has forced itself on me throughout my whole teaching career in my work on both the New Testament and church history. This fundamental conception is that every Christian confession has a permanent spiritual gift, a charisma, which it should preserve, nurture, purify, and deepen, and which should not be given up for the sake of homogenization. My many encounters with Christians of other confessions and my experiences in their worship services have repeatedly confirmed this impression and strengthened my conviction that the one church of Christ is present in a special form as the body of Christ in every Christian confession. This fact is to be kept in view in all our strivings toward ecumenicity.

This perspective is not secondary for me; rather, it is the primary perspective from which I view ecumenical problems. It could appear that from this point of view I might arrive at a solution to the problem of unity that is lacking in courage and all too modest, or even that I am fostering the kind of ecumenical stagnation about which people are currently complaining. In response, I can only reaffirm that with this publication I wish to counteract such ecumenical pessimism. I intend to indicate that my concept of Christian unity does not at all call for "everything to remain as is."

I know that, in my intentions, I am in agreement with the authors of other ecumenical models, although they think that these models are to be actualized in differing ways. This is why I am concerned to set forth my understanding within the context of recent discussions. For this reason I will first mention some recent works with which I, along with others, especially enter into discussion and debate.

As I prepared my lecture for the Week of Prayer for Christian Unity, "Ökumenismus der Einheit in der Vielheit nach dem Neuen Testament" (The Ecumenism of Unity through Diversity according to the New Testament; chap. 1 of this book),[1] given in the St. Peter's Church in Basel in January 1984, Heinrich Fries and Karl Rahner's book, *Unity of the Churches: An Actual Possibility*,[2] was not yet available to me. On the other hand, the esteemed Catholic theologian Karl Rahner, who had died in the meantime, and his co-author and close associate in Munich, Heinrich Fries, could not at that time have known of my Basel lecture. Their concept of ecumenicity and mine have points of contact although developed independently, and they are borne by a common will to unity. The two proposals, however, rest on different foundations and have a different orientation with regard to the ultimate goal of the unity for which we strive. To bring my proposal, which proceeds from the New Testament, into dialogue with the significant concept of the two Catholic theologians appears to me to be all the more in the interests of the common cause, since a lively discussion has developed around *Unity of the Churches*,[3] a discussion in which I am participating in any case. I was able to refer in my lecture to the important work of the Lutheran systematic theologian E. Schlink which appeared at the end of 1983.[4]

Since my original lecture was composed, other ecumenical efforts have blossomed that need to be surveyed. Ecumenical dialogues in the commissions between the representatives of the different churches have been decidedly advanced. There have been bilateral discussions between Roman Catholics and the Lutheran,[5] the Anglican, and the Orthodox churches—each separate from the other—as well as general interconfessional cooperative work, from which the "Lima document" had already appeared in 1982.[6] This document has been and is the subject of continuing studies. The papal office as an ecumenical problem has lately been discussed in many joint publications, most recently by a group of well-known theologians of different confessions.[7] On another level, the Neuenburg professor Jean-Louis Leuba,[8] who has long pursued an ecumenical line similar to mine, though developed independently, has carried on a literary discussion with a representative of the Taizé community concerning the special way to Christian unity proposed by this community.[9] The story of the relations between the World Council of Churches (WCC) and the Roman Catholic Church was told by the esteemed Secretary of that Geneva institution, W. A. Visser't Hooft, in a manuscript completed a few days before his death.[10] The story stretches from the beginnings of the WCC in 1914 to 1984, is full of ups and downs, and portrays not only the great difficulties experienced by the relationship of the two bodies, but also its fruitfulness.

This year has also seen the appearance of the book of Cardinal J. Ratzinger, *The Ratzinger Report*.[11] The book grew out of an interview, and has already evoked considerable debate. Shortly before completing my manuscript, I received from Cardinal H. de Lubac a book about the Second Vatican Council that is likewise based on an interview.[12] This book receives its particular importance with regard to the synod Pope John Paul II convened and devoted to this Council. Although ecumenism is mentioned only in passing, it illuminates the efforts toward unity which come into consideration in the present situation. After the completion of my manuscript, and immediately before sending it to the press, I had the opportunity to see the issue of the *Ökumenischen Forum* dedicated to Prof. W. Gruber (Graz) on his sixtieth birthday. This work contains important essays.[13]

I acknowledge all these recent publications for my work in this book. In chapter 1, however, I reproduce my above-mentioned lecture, in response to requests from Basel, Paris, and Rome, approximately in its original form derived from my engagement with the New Testament. It appears to me most appropriate to present in this manner the foundational work for the practical realization of my conception. Where necessary, I bring the remarks contained in my lecture into relation with the recent literature mentioned above, in footnotes and excursuses which were added later. Since the center of gravity of this book lies in chapter 1, I ask the reader not to read chapters 2 and 3 without paying careful attention to this first chapter.

In chapter 2 I have attempted to deal at length with the difficult issue of the practical realization of unity through diversity, especially its structural aspects, which I only touched on in my lecture.

In chapter 3 I respond, from the point of view of my proposal and in very summary form, to the conceptions of my ecumenical dialogue partners and to the practical consequences of their conceptions, some of which are in agreement with mine and some of which are not. It is inevitable that my attempt at a solution will evoke much opposition on both sides of the discussion. But this will serve the cause of unity, if, as I dare to hope, it will be a matter of constructive, edifying criticism from the authorized representatives of the ecclesiastical and theological communities.

I here express my gratitude to all who have helped me in their variety of ways, above all to Pastor G. Schwinn in Pirmasens and especially to the tried-and-true press of J. C. B. Mohr (Paul Siebeck), whose work means so much not only for theology in general, but especially for ecumenism.

For the sake of simplicity, I have used "Catholic" to mean "Roman Catholic."

The scholarly vice of frequent quotation of one's own works I have attempted to avoid when possible, but such references were still necessary more often that I would have wished.

I have perhaps referred to articles in Festschriften more than usual, since they contain important subject matter, and since significant articles, which represent a sacrifice of time for their authors and the most valuable kind of birthday presents for those to whom they are presented, should not, as is often the case, remain "buried" and forgotten in these anthologies.

OSCAR CULLMAN
New Year's Day 1986

I

The Ecumenism of Unity through Diversity according to the New Testament

ECUMENISM HAS BECOME FASHIONABLE in many circles today. Every good thing which becomes fashionable is in danger of losing its essential element, especially by oversimplification, by minimizing its inherent problems. In the following, I would like to distinguish what I consider true ecumenism from that which appears to me to be false. In this, I will use the New Testament as the criterion for deciding between "true" and "false."

The challenge of ecumenism can be expressed in one word: "unity." The oversimplification of this task is seen when unity is understood to mean the same as uniformity or enforced conformity. "Una sancta" is not the same as "uniformitas sancta." In order to avoid this false equation, we must define unity more precisely as "unity in plurality," in a manner which understands plurality not only quantitatively, but also qualitatively in the sense of diversity.[1] But this plurality can be understood from another perspective to mean a mere multiplicity without any inherent relationships, a kind of plurality which only leads to fragmentation and splits. "Plurality" must therefore be defined more carefully as "plurality in unity." Both concepts, unity and plurality, must be taken with complete seriousness!

Most theologians who are concerned with ecumenicity declare that they agree in principle with the concept of "unity in plurality," so it could appear that I am pushing against doors that are already open. But, on the one hand, this understanding has not everywhere penetrated the so-called average membership of the different confessions, which seems rather to expect that a complete uniformity would be forced upon all churches, often in indifference to or even disdain for questions of faith. On the other hand, many advocates of ecumenism agree with the concept of unity in plurality, but consider it a temporary state of affairs, which in the distant future would have to yield to a merger that would fuse the churches into one uniform body. Others are ready to acknowledge an ultimate unity in most areas, but they do not extend this unity to include denominational structures, or do so only in a limited degree.

Y. Congar, who always raises essential questions, in *Möglichkeiten* has also done so with regard to my rectoral address at the University of Basel ("Die ökumenische Aufgabe heute im Lichte der Kirchengeschichte," Basel, 1968). At the time I had already offered the prospect of the peaceful coexistence of the Catholic and non-Catholic churches based on the complementarity of their spiritual gifts, but had not yet developed it more precisely, as here. His question: is the prospect thought of as a temporary arrangement or as the final state? Congar infers from the fact that in that speech I described this friendly coexistence as "the *present* ecumenical task" (p. 24), emphasizing the word "present," that I was there suggesting only a preliminary state of affairs, but that in the long run I, like he, could not be satisfied with the continuing existence of two churches. In that speech I used the word "present," however, with reference to the irenic confrontation of the peculiarities of the differing confessions, not in contrast to a later disappearance of their charismatic diversity, but in contrast to the circumstance mentioned in the preceding sentence of the polemical debates concerning these differences in the past. Although unlike Congar I neither at that time had a temporary status in mind, nor do I have such a view today, I am in agreement with him that peaceful coexistence, *as it exists today*, is not adequate. I am here presenting my case precisely with the intention of getting beyond the present situation and establishing the unity of the churches in and through their diversity. To be sure, there remains a difference between us. The bond of unity sought by me is not, as for Congar, a united church as the body of Christ, but a less exacting "community of churches," which is not as such the body of Christ, but which would clarify and guarantee that the one church as the body of Christ is visibly manifest in each of the individual partner churches.

For Fries-Rahner too, the ultimate goal is not a "fusion." But the formulation of Thesis II (p. 35), "This is left to a broader consensus in the future" (see also Fries, p. 166), does raise questions in this regard which will be dealt with below (pp. 52–53 and 68). The understanding of the Orthodox churches comes close to my own. On this, see especially G. Larentzakis, "Vielheit in der Einheit aus der Sicht der orthodoxen Kirche," *Ök. Forum* 8 (1985): 65ff.

The "ecumenical impatience"[2] ("things are simply not progressing fast enough") that is found so often today and is so disadvantageous for the cause of unity derives from a false goal. This must necessarily lead to failure and disappointment. On the other hand, the expectation of merger misleads one into underestimating the value of the progress which has been experienced since the last Council—amazing progress after centuries of separation, progress from which it is not possible to retreat. The very different ecumenical situation of only a few decades ago is too easily forgotten.[3] It is certainly true that there have been no spectacular developments, as one with a perverted expectation of a merger might have expected. But the progress which has been made is lasting, and brings us nearer to a true unity in diversity.

Even if there is much talk today of the stagnation and regression of the ecumenical movement (not altogether unjustified), this is the fault—not exclusively, but in great part—of a false understanding of ecumenism based on a utopian hope, which can only generate paralyzing discouragement. I am therefore concerned here to raise a warning concerning the causes of this false hope.

What I advocate, not as a preliminary state, but as an ultimate goal of all our strivings toward unity, is a union of all Christian churches within which each would preserve its valuable elements, including its structure. Lacking a better expression ("alliance"?), I have called this a "federation" (in contrast to merger), despite the fact that the word in its secular sense is not adequate.

Since I have learned that much of the audience who heard my lecture objected to this term, I prefer to drop it, although I so far have not been able to find a completely adequate substitute. This terminological issue is no problem for Fries-Rahner, since they have in view a church which would be composed of the partner churches. J.-L. Leuba has proposed "amphictyony" ("Ökumenische Amphiktyonie" in Möglichkeiten, 86). Although this word would appropriately describe the thing intended, it appears to me not to be appropriate, since it would often be misunderstood (especially in view of the decline of classical education). It will probably be best to be satisfied with the expression "community of churches," although it is less precise. On this, see below (pp. 35–36 and 72–73). It has the advantage of taking into consideration the connotations of the term "communio," the ecumenical importance of which has been pointed out by Cardinal J. Willebrands, "L'avenir de l'oecuménisme," Proche Orient (1975): 3–15, and P. Duprey in his precise analytical essay "La communion ecclesiale" (a lecture presented to the congress of the Société internationale de Droit canonique oriental in Geneva, Sept. 16, 1985).

As a result of a misunderstanding for which I am responsible, at the end of the Italian edition of my lecture (in Protestantesimo 40 [1985]: 139), the words "chiesa multiforme e a appunto per questo chiesa una," which originally stood in the manuscript, but which I later placed in brackets in order to indicate that they were to be omitted, were nevertheless printed, in brackets.

From the very beginning, in order to avoid misunderstandings, I would like to emphasize that my extremely positive valuation of confessional diversity is in no way intended to minimize the great significance of common ecumenical worship services and common texts concerning theologically important issues such as church, Baptism, Eucharist, and ministerial office.[4] They should rather be expanded, but only to the point where the particular charismatic gifts of the different churches are threatened with becoming indistinct or suppressed. We will see that there are, of course, peculiarities to be weeded out, namely those that are distortions of the charismatic gifts. They should neither be passed over in silence nor minimized. But they are to be distinguished from those which not only are no hindrance to unity, but also enrich it. It should not be a matter of unity in spite of diversity, but of unity in diversity, or even better: unity *through* diversity.

This is what I would like to emphasize in the following discussions, in the light of the New Testament foundations of all true efforts for unity. That is, I would like for the discussion to be illuminated by (1) the New Testament understanding of the Holy Spirit; (2) (closely related to the preceding) the New Testament understanding of the work of the Holy Spirit as producing diversity through the gifts, the charisms, that are conferred in every confession; (3) the ranking offered by the New Testament for the statements of faith proclaimed by each confession, that is, the so-called hierarchy of truths; (4) the concept of salvation history, to the extent that the biblical revelation is developed in this mode.

1. Ecumenism and the Holy Spirit

To create unity belongs to the essential nature of the Holy Spirit (Pentecost). Apart from the Holy Spirit, no ecumenism is possible! But we also discover that where the Holy Spirit is at work in accord with its true nature, diversifying plurality is generated within this unity.[5] It would be helpful here to reflect on 1 Cor. 12:4–31. Here Paul shows clearly that the Holy Spirit creates unity not only in spite of diversity, but precisely *through* it. The apostle uses the image of our body. The church called into life by the Holy Spirit is an organism in which, as in the human body, each member contributes to the formation of a united structure precisely on the basis of its particular structure and function. Paul points out that one organic unity is formed through the fact that the foot does not perform the same function as the hand, and vice versa. It is the very nature of the Holy Spirit to function *so as to create diversity*. But this does not cause fragmentation, since every member is oriented to the goal of the unity of the whole body; it is the same with the members of the church. The richness of the full measure of the Holy Spirit consists in this plurality. Whoever does not respect this richness, and wants uniformity instead, sins against the Holy Spirit.[6]

My extension of the meaning of 1 Corinthians 12 to the unity of the church has of course met with the proper exegetical objection that Paul does not have churches in view here, but only individual members of the congregation. But the application to churches is certainly in accord with the apostle's meaning. For if we take into consideration the whole corpus of his letters, we discover that he also ascribes a particular mission to each of the different churches. In Rom. 1:11 he expresses his desire to visit the church in Rome (which had not been founded by him) with a view to a mutual "strengthening in the Spirit." He obviously is thinking here of his enrichment by the special spiritual gift, the charism, of the congregation which had developed in the capital of the empire. He likewise speaks of the one "church, which is in Corinth" (1 Cor. 1:2). This of course expresses his view that the same *one* church is present in Corinth: thus an expression of the church's unity. But at the very same time, it is precisely *this* church—located in *this* particular place, in connection with *this* situation and the problems involved in it—which has maintained its particular charismatic commission. The same is true of Thessalonica, Galatia, Philippi, Ephesus, and so forth. We thus have an expression of the church's diversity. In every individual church, and precisely in its particularity, the one church, the body of Christ, is present. That is the greatness of the work of the Holy Spirit. We will see[7] that different groups existed from the very beginnings of the church.

The denial of the work of the Holy Spirit has two opposite results, each of which is equally fateful for the cause of Christian unity: on the one side an anarchic *(anarchisch)* ecumenism, and on the other side its exact counterpart, a hardening of confessional barriers that excludes any hope for unity. Both attitudes—and they are both present in our activities these days—oppose the work of the Holy Spirit. On the one hand the spirit of anarchy resists the Holy Spirit that works at the same time for both diversity and order. The Holy Spirit is also the creator of order (1 Cor. 14:33, 40) and has nothing in common with that hasty, fanatical destruction of those distinctive organic features of a particular body that have grown under its influence. Fanatical, violent lust for progress is not inspired by the Holy Spirit, but by a completely different spirit.[8] The opposite result is obtained by understanding unity to mean uniformity, which leads to so-called integrism (*Integrismus*). This also, in its own way, disdains the work of the Holy Spirit as we have described it. It sees the work of the Spirit only in its own confession, not in the others. So the Catholic "integrists" call for a "return" of the others "to the bosom" of the mother church; the Protestant "integrists"—for there are such—proceed from the false view that the Holy Spirit has completely withdrawn from the churches which did not join the Reformation of the sixteenth century, so they can only regard unity as a matter of inviting the Catholics to convert to Protestantism. In neither case can one any longer speak of ecumenicity.[9]

When we consciously and consistently seek to attain unity in diversity, we by no means make the ecumenical task any easier. On the contrary, when we keep the spiritual gifts in view, the difficult question emerges: How are these to be distinguished from their distortions, and how is their mutual recognition in the different confessions to be actualized?

2. Ecumenism and Charisma

"Varieties of gifts, but the same Spirit," writes Paul in 1 Cor. 12:4, and in the following verses he lists these gifts—named "charisms" from the Greek word for grace. His understanding of the church created by the Spirit is entirely based on this fundamental truth of the variety of charisms. In the parable of the Talents in Matt. 25:14–30 the emphasis is of course placed on the task that is given along with the gift, but also in Matthew the variety of gifts is presupposed, all of which are equally valued.

Each charism bestowed by the Spirit is exposed to the danger of being distorted by other spirits, and thus becoming a source of heresy. Only the charism free of distortion, not its perversion, can contribute to the richness of the diversity of the community of churches for which we are striving. In this regard, a self-critical stance should be required of all churches. They should be constantly ready to weed out perversions. This is not only an innerchurch necessity, but also, and especially, an ecumenical necessity.[10] Because people in each church are disposed to see only the distortion of the charism in the other church, and not the charism itself, they incorrectly suppose that in order to have unity each church must give up its peculiarities. But struggle against the perversion should not lead to throwing the baby out with the bath water.

If the charisms were to be given up in favor of a uniformity, the result would be an anemic structure, a false appearance of unity, which would have little in common with that entity created by the Spirit which the New Testament calls "church."[11] Then the danger emerges that unity would be constructed on the basis of some sort of ideal, not taken from the Bible, but perhaps purely political. The impressive prayer of Jesus in John 17:11, "that they all may be one," may not be so understood that unity is to be attained at any price, even at the price of the charisms.[12] That would mean, to use a word of Jesus, driving out the devil by Beelzebub, eliminating division by destroying the entrusted talents.

Although every church must give its own account for its own charisms and the danger of their perversion, it still belongs inherently to ecumenical dialogue that candid, brotherly (and sisterly) conversations take place concerning what members of one church believe they see in their sister churches. Even while the sister church has itself not set aside the distortions of its own charisms, fellowship with it should nonetheless not be diminished. The confessions should meet each other at the level of their own charisms, not their distortions, and not with the goal of imitating each other—imitation leads to superficiality and trivializing of the charisms.[13] Each church is to respect and learn from the charisms of the other in order to deepen[14] the church's own charisms, to purify them, and to guard them against perversion. This mutuality in learning means that the first question may not be (as is so often the case, especially among us theologians) "What can I criticize or combat in the other's position?" but "Where can and must I recognize and use that which is positive?" Then, but not until then, may I of course also ask: "What, since it is a distortion, can I not take over from the other, what must I clearly reject for the sake of the truth, because I believe that I find a distortion there?"[15] This is the view of the apostle, when in 1 Thess. 5:19–21, a passage dealing explicitly with the Spirit, he writes: "Do not quench the Spirit, do not despise prophesying, but test everything; hold fast what is good." By using the Greek verb *dokimazein* ("to test") Paul is not here saying, "criticize everything," but "examine everything." The spiritual gifts of the different churches should be cultivated again, not trimmed away for the sake of uniformity, and also not imitated. They should rather be activated afresh in order to supplement each other.

In the following, I will attempt, in very summary fashion, to determine the essential charisms of the churches which derived from the Reformation of the sixteenth century and those of the Catholic churches.[16] In this we will take for granted that an especially developed charism in one church is not altogether lacking in the other, but only that it is not characteristic of it. I thus name as a Protestant charism *concentration on the Bible*, on the one hand, and *freedom*, on the other, which fosters openness to the world[17] and also determines the structure of the Protestant churches. The essential charisms of the Catholic Church are, on the one hand, *universalism*, in the spatial and temporal sense (legitimate tradition),[18] and, on the other, the *institution*, the organization, which makes it possible for it to speak authoritatively to its members and to the world, and which despite possible variations establishes unified orders.[19] To the extent that organization is a charism, it of course serves as a safeguard for the Spirit (1 Cor. 14:33, 40). As charisms of the Orthodox church I would mention especially the theological deepening of the concept of the Spirit on the one hand, and on the other the conservation of traditional liturgical forms.

Like all charisms, these too are constantly threatened with distortion. Thus the Protestant charism of concentration on the Bible, when pushed too far, becomes too narrow, so that measured by the richness of the gospel the result is "too little." This distortion may emerge, for example, when elements that are not explicitly mentioned in the Bible but which are thoroughly in accord with its spirit are omitted or even resisted. Things such as meditation and contemplation[20] come to mind, as do many matters related to worship, since many of the elements which were still present in the time of the Reformation fell victim to the secularization process of later centuries—except for Scandinavian Lutheranism and the Anglican Church. One could even mention the absence of at least some form of the teaching office (which would of course have a different form in Protestantism than the Catholic form of the office). The lack of any sort of teaching office can lead to a pluralism which within the Protestant churches amounts to a crippling fragmentation. The other Protestant charism, that of Christian *freedom* (along with openness to the world), can likewise lose its character as a charism, namely when freedom dissolves into anarchy, where neither institution nor order is considered essential, when it is forgotten that God is "not a God of confusion" (1 Cor. 14:33) and that "all things should be done decently and in order" (1 Cor. 14:40). On the other hand, openness to the world can become uncritical subjection to the world (Rom. 12:2), in which the substance of the Christian faith is lost. In this case false accommodation to the world's new morality, especially in a decadent period, leads to a disintegration of morality as has happened from time to time in the past and is unfortunately happening now. In such a situation the gospel is accommodated to the currently dominant morality, and not morality to the gospel, and human weaknesses are not forgiven, as in the gospel, but are justified.

On the Catholic side, the charisms are also exposed to the danger of distortion. The charisma of universalism, radiating the gospel throughout the whole world, can lead to a temptation for Catholicism in connection with the claim that it alone possesses and guarantees the "fullness" of the gospel, a claim backed up by the appeal to divine right founded on apostolic succession—an appeal which is not without its own problems. This understanding of Catholicity is an impediment for ecumenism in the perspective proposed here, within which the charisms of the different churches mutually supplement each other.

Even the pronouncement on ecumenism of the last Council, "Unitatis Redintegratio,"[21] so open to ecumenicity in other respects, emphasizes that the separated churches are important "means of salvation," but adds the supplementary statement that they "derive their efficacy from the very fullness of grace and truth entrusted in the Catholic Church." Prominent Catholic theologians have recognized this extreme formulation of the concept of catholicity, and have given it up, as in the remarkable discussion in Fries-Rahner (p. 48): in comparison with the realities which other churches have brought forth, "the Roman Catholic church in fact exhibits deficiencies." In the same passage Fries-Rahner cite an amazing statement in this regard made by Pope John Paul II in a speech during the 1980 anniversary celebration of the Augsburg Confession. According to Fries-Rahner the statement was not actually made by him, but was present in his written outline: "The Spirit of God has allowed us to recognize anew that as long as the church has not realized the fullness of its God-willed catholicity there are authentic elements of Catholicism existing outside its visible community" (pp. 48–49).

Further, the charism of universality is threatened by the danger of what is called syncretism, this mixing of authentic Christian elements with alien, unassimilable elements, with the result that the different parts are no longer controlled and held together by the fundamental truth of the gospel. From here it can proceed to the same false secularism which we have found as a distorting element in Protestantism.[22]

But it remains the case that the danger of Protestantism is in this regard that of "too little," while for Catholicism it is that of "too much." The other Catholic charism I have mentioned, that of organization, of institution, can be distorted to become institutionalism and totalitarianism,[23] in which the Spirit is stifled, while the charism of institution is given for precisely the opposite purpose, namely to guard the Spirit with a protective wall as a safeguard against anarchistic excesses of rank outgrowths.

As distortions of the Orthodox charisms I would think of something like rigidity and formalism.

A warning against the distortion of the charisms appears to me to be especially necessary, for it is these distortions which create divisions, while the charisms themselves create unity precisely through their diversity.[24]

The multiplicity of kinds of charisms corresponds to the variety and plurality of the truths proclaimed by the different churches. The spiritual gifts set forth revelations of truth ("Spirit of truth," John 14:17; 15:26; 16:13). This poses an especially important problem for the ecumenical discussion, that of the hierarchy of truths, a hierarchy which is not the same in the separated churches of today.

3. The "Hierarchy of Truths"

In the decree of Vatican II on ecumenism, "Unitatis Redintegratio" ("Decree on Ecumenism"), the necessity of a *ranking* of the confessional statements of faith is explicitly acknowledged. That is one of the achievements of the Council so important for the ecumenical dialogue. Even if not absolutely new, it receives a significance not previously attained precisely by the place in which it appeared.[25] It is to be noted that the different affirmations are, to be sure, all kept as binding truths,[26] but instead of standing on an even status with each other, as previously, they now are ranked from the top down. Foundational dogmas are distinguished from those that are derived, the purpose of the latter being to develop and explain the former, and to make them more precise. As interpretative elaborations, the derived dogmas are also binding if they are proclaimed as dogmas by the church, but they do not receive the priority attributed to the foundational dogmas. The acknowledgment of a ranking removes some of the sharpness of the controversies which continue concerning the remaining divergences, namely, if the controversies concern dogmas which no longer stand at or near the top. To name one possible example: the christological dogmas have a higher ranking than the Marian dogmas, without these latter losing their truth value within Catholicism.[27]

The churches which derive from the Reformation of the sixteenth century also acknowledge—though only implicitly, to be sure—that the truths which they proclaim can be ranked in a certain hierarchy. The scale by which such truths are distinguished and ranked, a scale which is present in all churches, is different from church to church.[28] But in this respect too, a diversity grounded in the distinctions among real charisms can be accepted and even regarded as an enrichment of the church. Let us think, for example, of the high evaluation placed on the doctrine of the Holy Spirit among the teachings of the Orthodox churches.

But this may only happen under the indispensable condition that a common complex of foundational dogmas (within the picture provided by hierarchical language, a common apex) is accepted by all the churches included in the community of churches we are trying to achieve. Without the bond provided by this condition, the pluralism of confessional statements would lead only to fragmentation.

But how are these foundational truths which constitute the apex to be determined? Loyal to their concentration on the Bible, Protestants are inclined to answer: they are to be obtained through the Bible (as though that made any further discussion unnecessary). But that would be too simple. In reality, Protestantism too must concern itself with this question, since we are here placed before the problem of the "canon within the canon." History shows that among the teachings revealed in the Bible, sometimes one and sometimes another has been exalted to the role of the primary truth by means of which all other truths are to be explained. For Erasmus this was the Sermon on the Mount (Matthew 5–7), for the Reformers the Pauline doctrine of justification, for the Orthodox churches the Johannine theology. Martin Luther recognized the difficulty, and in the preface to his commentary on the Epistles of James presented the decisive principle as "what preaches (or, urges) Christ" (was Christum treibet). But this rule, though correct in itself, is too vague.

In order to find an objective criterion for the precise establishment of the primary truth within the Bible, I am accustomed to referring to the credal statements which were already recorded in fixed form within early Christianity and were cited by the authors of the New Testament themselves as the quintessence of their faith. It was with this intention that I wrote my study of the oldest Christian confessions of faith.[29] By means of these short summary statements, early Christianity declared and preserved what it considered to be essential. But here too, I add: without thereby making superfluous the other truths of revelation to which it testified. They accented some items. These confessions of faith often consist of a short clause, such as "Christ is the Lord" *(Kyrios Christos)*. Others are more developed. Thus in 1 Cor. 15:3–8 and Phil. 2:6–11 Paul quotes credal statements which had already been developed in early Christianity and were used primarily in worship. In 1 Cor. 15:3 the apostle explicitly explains that the following enumeration of fundamental savings acts had been previously transmitted to him in the tradition ("For I delivered to you as of first importance what I also received, that . . ."). From it proceeded the creeds of the later church. From these oldest New Testament summaries of the faith we can infer which statements about Christ among those which, to use Luther's words, "preach Christ" receive the highest valuation: the death of Christ and above all, his resurrection and exaltation (the "present Lord"). The faith in the creator God (the first article of the later creed) is presupposed as self-evident by the Old Testament, the only Bible of the early church. Thus it is not particularly mentioned in the majority of New Testament formulae, since it was not a specifically distinctive mark of the early Christians.

In determining the apex of the hierarchy of truths, may we go further without as Protestants becoming disloyal to the charism of biblical concentration? The question is to be answered in the affirmative, which allows us to incorporate the more developed confessional statements of the church of the first few centuries. These confessional statements are regarded by almost all churches as correct and legitimate developments of the biblical revelation. It is extraordinarily important that the Reformers accepted them as such; this acknowledgment is a corrective to the danger to which the biblical principle is so exposed, that of a narrowing which leads to distortions. By means of these credal statements, there can be an overcoming of the objection "too little" with regard to the use of the Bible alone. But I would propose that from the Catholic side too it could be accepted that alongside the more developed creeds of early Christianity there could be placed the most important New Testament formulae. These are all the stronger because of their abbreviated concentration, especially since the later creeds contain longer statements and thus make emphases which, if not absolutely necessary, are still very useful.[30] It is to be noted that

Karl Rahner, the preeminent Catholic theologian who recently died, suggested as a common point of reference the baptismal confession called the "Apostles' Creed," and the creed of Nicaea-Constantinople, that is, the creed of the mass (fourth century).[31] Both are accepted by almost all churches, and also used in the worship services of most churches. Thus there exists today an ecumenically promising situation with regard to primary truth.[32]

Differences remain between the churches, however; differences which concern the truths derived from the apex. Along with their relative rank on the scale, there is also the problem that some series of confessional statements contain affirmations that are entirely lacking in other series. This is a problem which may not be simply ignored. It is related to the danger of "too much" and "too little." Here one must examine, from the one side, whether the presence of the affirmation in question is legitimate; that is, whether it really is derived from the primary truth accepted in common, or whether it has no connection to the primary truth, but stems from a teaching foreign to it. From the other side, one must examine whether what we have suggested above with regard to the institutions and liturgical elements lacking in Protestantism is also true with regard to the corresponding *elements of doctrine*, namely, that without being explicitly mentioned in the Bible, they still stand in implicit harmony with it and are able to illuminate the primary truth. In principle, the first could be an example of "too much" by the Catholics, and the last an example of "too little" by the Protestants, so that the individual affirmations are to be examined on both sides.

With regard to that ticklish theme of Mariology which burdens the Catholic-Protestant dialogue, I only raise here the one question: Is it really possible that all the Marian dogmas can be regarded as developments from the confessional statements of the ancient church about conception by the Holy Spirit and birth from the Virgin Mary? J. Ratzinger (*Ratzinger Report*, 106ff.) with reference to the Second Vatican Council, strongly emphasizes the anchoring of Mariology in Christology, even as he also affirms the "clear" (p. 106) biblical grounding of all four Marian dogmas. But is not the circuitous path from the dogma of the bodily assumption of Mary to heaven back to the statements of the New Testament (and the ancient Christian confessions) entirely too long to permit us today to regard this dogma as a "development"? The great length of time involved in the development is after all quite important in this case. Is not the significance of the description of Christ as the "firstborn of the dead" (*prototokos*, Col. 1:18; Rev. 1:5), as the "first fruits" (*aparche*, 1 Cor. 15:20, 23), diminished by this dogma, especially since in 1 Cor. 15:23 between the resurrection of Christ as the "first fruits" and the bodily resurrection of "those who belong to Christ at his coming" there is no room left for an intermediary anticipation of this by the bodily assumption of Mary (v. 23—*epeita*: then, afterward).

A concern for the truth will not allow this question to be suppressed. Similarly, there is the question of whether damage is done to the primary truth of Christology by the place given to Mary in Catholic theology, that is the amount of space which it gives to Mary, and the nearness to Christ in which she is placed.

Despite these unavoidable questions, the fact remains that the hierarchy of truths acknowledged by the last Council implies a *distinction in rank* between the primary truth and the derived truths implied by it. The remaining divergence between the Catholic and the Protestant attitude to this problem can at least be moderated by the fact that from the Protestant side there is an effort to find a positive charismatic nucleus in Mariology. The Reformers obviously rejected only the Marian cult, but not great respect for the Virgin Mary. See W. Tappolet and A. Ebneter, *Das Marienlob der Reformatoren* (Tübingen: Katzmann-Verlag, 1962). With regard to Luther, see now the very thorough work of B. Gherardini, *Lutero-Maria. Pro o contra?* (Pisa: Giardini, 1985).

Among the positive aspects of Mariology can be counted the high evaluation of chastity and of motherhood implicit in it.

It is also the case that a doctrine accepted as authentic Christian truth by all churches, and which thus unquestionably belongs to the church's proclamation, can be a hindrance for the realization of a community of different churches. This can happen if such a doctrine is so strongly overemphasized that it becomes a second apex of the hierarchy of truths, or even threatens to usurp the place of the true apex. The harmony of the gospel is then destroyed.[33] Thus, for example, the revelation of the ultimate end of all things is a constituent part of the gospel. But in many eschatological-apocalyptic sects it is so overemphasized that it ceases to fulfill properly the function appropriately assigned to it in the New Testament, with the result that the primary truth of the gospel is overshadowed by it. But only when this sort of eschatological expectation (often including calculation of the date) claims *absolute* priority is the acceptance of those sects which advocate it within the community of churches placed in question. But if the primary truth of the gospel remains intact, even if clouded by this shift of perspective, then a union with such groups is not excluded and a dialogue becomes not only possible, but also certainly necessary.[34] An analogous situation is in any case not limited to sectarian groups, but can also emerge within traditional churches if certain of their characteristic doctrines are pressed too far.

With regard to all the remaining divergences, whether their claim to belong within the realm of Christian truths at all is at issue, or whether it is merely a matter of their ranking within the scale of acknowledged Christian truths, Paul can show us how they belong to the one church despite these problems. He does it in response to a question which belongs to the former category; namely, with regard to the observation of ritual prescriptions concerning purity and dietary regulations which had incorrectly assumed a leading place in the faith of certain groups (as in Corinth). Here it is a matter of different practices in how one conducts one's life. But theological differences stand behind this difference in practice. Paul teaches the liberation from these prescriptions through Christ, by rejecting the theological approach of those whose faith is bound to those prescriptions and proscriptions. But despite his conviction concerning the truth of freedom in Christ, he calls for loving consideration for the brothers and sisters whom he characterizes as "weak in faith."

Although the issue dealt with here is not of fundamental importance for Paul, since the "weakness" in this case obviously does not impair the primary truth of the gospel, this call for tolerance is still for him an extremely important concern. He thus discusses it extensively several times: 1 Cor. 8:4–13; 10:19—11:1; Rom. 14:1—15:13. He wants the faith of that brother or sister for whom Christ died to suffer no damage (Rom. 14:15). The awareness of freedom should not play a superior role to love—in the realm of ethics too, there is a ranking with regard to what is more and less important. The apostle here shows us the path we must follow in order to be able to walk together *even when differences cannot be overcome.* The Pauline concept of "weakness in the faith" presents an appropriate model for the conduct of the separated churches even in regard to issues which, from our point of view, are more important concerns than those discussed by Paul.

Among these concerns would be those remaining distortions of the charisms which we think we see among our sister churches (see above, p. 19).

The Pauline tolerance based on the concept of "weakness in faith" appears to me to be preferable to the "withholding of judgment" (or the postponement of a consensus until later) proposed by Fries-Rahner in the discussion of their Thesis II. In Paul's view concern for the truth of the matter requires that, despite all the tolerance exercised, one must not remain silent concerning the contradiction involved. Jüngel ("Ein Schritt voran") extends the concept of "adiaphora," originally used with regard to church practices, to the statements by Fries-Rahner in their Thesis II. To be sure, Fries (p. 165) rejects the application of this concept to these statements, since they also have to be acknowledged as containing truth. On "adiaphora," see the book by Herms (*Einheit der Christen*).

Among those ecumenical divergences represented by items present among the important doctrines of one group but lacking in another group, divergences which from a human point of view are hardly to be overcome, should we list the Petrine office (*Petrusamt*) which Fries (p. 174) calls "a still unresolved problem"? We will discuss this in chapter 2 of this work. The same question is to be raised with regard to the concept of the "church," which according to Ratzinger (*Ratzinger Report*, 106) stands as a divergence of insuperable difficulty between Catholics and Protestants. (See also pp. 77–79 below.)

To be sure, a difficulty is presented by the fact that the emphasizing of a particular affirmation is considered a mark of the "strong" in one church, while in another church the "strong" consider the rejection of this same affirmation to be their characteristic mark, and vice versa. But nonetheless the demand of the apostle still applies, to accept with love those described as "weak" by one side or the other.

But of course the condition remains in force that all sides not abandon the common foundation which we have described as the primary truth of the gospel. Here is the boundary of the tolerance demanded by Paul. He does not confuse the "weak in faith" with those whom he designates in Galatians as "false brethren" (2:4) and to whom he makes no concessions at all (1:9). The same boundary should also be observed for the acceptance of certain sectarian groups.[35] The other Pauline command, which should stand at the beginning of all ecumenical striving, still applies, namely, not to forget that love always must be united with respect for the truth (Eph. 4:15).[36]

4. Salvation History as the Locus of the Development of Unity through Diversity

The recognition of the divine activity within history is of fundamental significance for genuine ecumenism.[37] For lack of a better expression, the believer uses the term "salvation history" (*Heilsgeschichte*) to refer to that line which crosses secular history and is a part of it, that stream of history which "comes from eternity, is made within time, and draws us towards eternity."[38] It is that stream of history reported in the

Bible.[39] In the New Testament, this history is played out within the two boundaries represented by John 1:1 ("In the beginning . . .") and 1 Cor. 15:28 (literally, " . . . God all in all"; RSV: " . . . that God may be everything to every one"). Only the salvation history recorded in the Bible is normative, but it is continued in certain events of general history. The identity of these events, however, can be attempted only very carefully, and from the point of view of the Bible. In all salvation history, a distinction is to be made between human contingency and continuity with the economy of salvation revealed in the Bible.[40] Salvation history thus includes non-salvation history *(Unheilsgeschichte)*, which, as a result of human sin, always resists the flow of the divine plan, but is still not able to destroy the continuity of the divine activity. Thus human jealousy, greed for power, and contentiousness are a constant threat to the divinely willed unity in diversity.

A false ecumenism which seeks merger confuses these two streams. It considers the historical origin of the different confessions and the resulting variety as such to be resistance to God, as merely an example of human bungling. Its goal is that abstract construction of which we have spoken, an abstraction remote from all that has actually developed in history. Leuba correctly designates the location of this sort of ecumenism as a kind of ecclesiastical "no man's land."[41]

There was no uniformity even in earliest Christianity. From the very beginning, we hear of different groups. We think of the group of "Hellenists" mentioned in Acts 6, and especially of the division of the apostolic preaching into two different missions, a Jewish-Christian mission and a Gentile-Christian mission, of which Paul speaks in Gal. 2:1–10. The multifaceted unity generated through the rich variety of tasks given through the Holy Spirit threatened a hostile split. But the Pauline report shows how the same early church was aware of this danger and knew how to avoid it, and that this was not through the construction of a uniformity achieved by compromise, but by a *separation* of the two missions with each acknowledging the "grace" conferred on the other (Gal. 2:9). The same God who is at work in the mission of Peter to preach the gospel to the Jews also stands behind Paul's worldwide preaching to the Gentiles (Gal. 2:8). As the symbol of "fellowship" it is further said (v. 9) that they "gave each other the right hand" and resolved to take a common collection for the poor, a project whose completion was a matter of concern for the apostle throughout his missionary career.

This New Testament institutionalization of the collection as the symbol of fellowship *(koinonia)*, of "unity in diversity," was the inspiration for my suggestion of a reciprocal collection. See my work *Message to Catholics and Protestants* (trans. Joseph A. Burgess [Grand Rapids: Wm. B. Eerdmans, 1959]) in which I proposed a collection by a Catholic church for the poor of a Protestant church, and a collection by a Protestant church for the poor of a Catholic church. In *Testimonia oecumenica* several fellow workers have raised the question as to why this proposal, which had been initially received with a certain enthusiasm (and was even especially well received by Cardinal E. Tisserant), and has experienced some happy results in both Catholic and Protestant congregations, has been allowed to sink into oblivion. (The large number of contributors who mention this suggestion is impressive—without being certain that I have not forgotten any, I note: Robert McAfee Brown, A. Ambrosanio, J. C. Bennett, Père Benoit, J. Burgess, M. Carrez, J. G. Fuchs, P. Geoltrain, E. Gritsch, K. F. Nickle, Cardinal Pellegrino, W. Rordorf, F. Trosch, V. Vinay. In *Möglichkeiten* [p. 107], J. H. Yoder also mentions it.) I fear that it is related to the fact that the suggestion was not correctly understood, and that especially its biblical basis (Gal. 2:7–10) as an expression of *unity* in *separation* was not taken into consideration. I have allowed myself to bring the matter up again because, as I will elaborate below (pp. 43–44), we only make progress in ecumenical solidarity when it finds some sort of concrete, even official expression.

This decision to respect diversity in unity made by the very first "Council," the so-called apostolic council, should set the direction for our own efforts toward unity in our different situation.

The parties at Corinth (1 Corinthians 1—4) are not a matter of unity through diversity but represent the kind of divisions caused by human weaknesses—especially since the factor of personality cults (Cephas, Paul, Apollos), which always causes fragmentation *(schismata,* 1 Cor. 1:10), plays a role, and since the unifying function of baptism (1 Cor. 12:13; Gal. 3:27) was not respected: "Were you baptized in the name of Paul?" (1 Cor. 1:13).

An example of charismatic, historical diversity is presented by the orders of monks founded in antiquity, the Middle Ages, and later, and which were structured and directed in very different ways. They were incorporated into the unity of the Catholic Church with their individual characteristic features, although the misapprehension of the charismatic character of the diversity also here sometimes led to all-too-human quarrels. Oriental churches that have united with Rome may likewise be named here, inasmuch as they have been allowed to preserve their characteristic features in the union.

But in order to preserve certain charisms in their pure form, it was perhaps also necessary that completely autonomous churches came into being (the Orthodox and the churches that derived from the Reformation). This would not necessarily and as such have led to a hostile separation which would have excluded every form of fellowship. In order to maintain a Christian fellowship *(koinonia)*, the "right hand of fellowship" could have been extended here too, despite the aspect of continuing separation, as at the apostolic council (cf. Gal. 2:9; Acts 15:1–31).

With remarkable insight the Bohemian Reformation which bears the Hussite stamp advocated precisely this New Testament understanding of unity through diversity and struggled for its realization: separation for the sake of the truth—reconciliation with *all* churches for the sake of unity. [Translator's note: There is a nuanced use of language here difficult to preserve in English: *Einigung/*"reconciliation," *Einheit/*"unity."] This is the real ecumenical concern of this branch of the Reformation from the fourteenth to the seventeenth century, when J. A. Comenius practically gives directions for the establishment of a "World Council of Churches."[42]

Generally speaking, the way of harmonious separation has not been trodden since then. From the very beginning, human sinfulness has transformed the richness of the church's diversity into hostile, fighting church groups and has even generated terrible persecutions and wars. That is the great historical sin of Christians. Our ecumenical assignment today does not consist in setting aside the diversity of the church which has its own theological significance from the point of view of the history of salvation, but rather of setting aside the scandalous non-salvation-history destruction of brotherly fellowship. We said at the beginning that unity cannot be uniformity, and here we add: difference, even separation, cannot be hostile separation.

Since in the past there has been such a close connection between legitimate diversity and human fault, the question could be raised whether henceforth any separation is evil in and of itself, and whether we should not strive for even more than the unification of separated churches, that is by resisting the continued existence of autonomous churches at all. But here history can teach us the lesson that even separated churches that currently exclude the possibility of their participation in any sort of merger can nevertheless fruitfully cross-fertilize one another, so that a union *in* the continuing separation becomes conceivable.

However great the human guilt may be for giving the separate existence of the churches a hostile character, nonetheless the continued existence of the Catholic Church, the Orthodox church, and the Reformation churches alongside each other has attained a certain meaning, both for Catholics and non-Catholics.[43] For Catholicism the existence of the Orthodox church and especially the Protestant churches was a sign, a warning, against distortion. From the Catholic side too it is hardly contested that the example of the non-Catholic churches has fostered certain reform movements within Catholicism. On the other hand, a historical understanding of the Reformation such as was previously only present in individual cases is now becoming generally accepted. It is now acknowledged that at that time a deplorable state of affairs had flawed the church. In the recent and current books on Luther by Catholic authors, as well as in the statements of Pope John Paul II concerning the reformer, his work and thought as well as his piety are evaluated in a remarkably positive manner. The positive papal declarations concerning the Lutheran Augsburg Confession also belong in this category.

On the other hand, the continued historical existence of the Catholic Church has often given the occasion for Protestants to ask themselves the already-noted question: should the many elements in harmony with the Bible that have been lost in the course of post-Reformation history due to the process of narrowing and false secularization—elements now only present in the Catholic (or Orthodox) churches—be recovered by the churches of the Reformation?

Faith in the divine activity may legitimately be expressed in the claim that good can come from a separation which occurred in a hostile fashion and which has resulted in much evil.[44] But such a faith cannot release us on either side from our ecumenical duty of resisting this evil, namely the causes of hostility (including the lack of mutual solidarity) between the churches and of seeking, respecting, and safeguarding the riches contained in the diversity of charisms, in order to place them in the service of unity.

Conclusion

I have presented for consideration only the main New Testament principles of an ecumenism of unity in charismatic diversity. That was the real subject of this discussion. For us the difficult question of the possibility of its practical realization remains to be resolved. I hope to accomplish this in the next chapter. I only wish to add one further comment here.

My remarks would be completely misunderstood if one concluded from them that I had the intention of suppressing ecumenical zeal, of fostering a kind of ecumenical paralysis, or of commending some sort of cheap ecumenism, since I reject the idea of actual merger. There is an encouraging will toward unity which can be found everywhere today as never before. I have presented my exposition of this subject precisely in order to safeguard it from disappointments and crippling failures that result from setting false goals. I resist the idea of merger not primarily because I consider it unrealistic and utopian—which it is, of course—but because it appears to me that this goal contradicts the nature of a true unity. What I propose is a real community of completely independent churches that remain Catholic, Protestant, and Orthodox, that preserve their spiritual gifts, not for the purpose of excluding each other, but for the purpose of forming a *community of all those churches that call on the name of our Lord Jesus Christ.*[45] We need to be seized by an unflagging zeal, not an ecumenical flash in the pan, which will give us the courage to take bold initiatives, but which will also not scorn the small steps that mean nothing to those who are panting after the false goal of homogenization, small steps that mean much for those who have the true goal before their eyes: a variety of gifts—one Spirit.

II

The Actualization of Unity through Diversity in Practice

IN THE PRECEDING DISCUSSION I have only mentioned in passing the question of the practical actualization of unity. I originally used the expression "federation" to designate the alternative to the idea of merger,[1] an alternative based on the New Testament concept of spiritual gifts. I have since abandoned the term "federation" because, on the one hand the secular use of the word led to misunderstandings and objections, and on the other hand it seemed to imply a structural solution. The possibility or impossibility of a structural solution must therefore be the subject of this chapter.

In order not to anticipate any particular conclusion, I have thus chosen the more general description "community of (harmoniously separated) churches." It leaves open the question of a comprehensive "superstructure" over the structures of the different denominations which would of course continue in effect. In the recently compiled document which concludes the latest phase of the bilateral conversations between the Catholic and the Lutheran churches, *Facing Unity*,[2] this terminology is also employed with reference to the planned community between the two churches, and can be extended without further ado to cover the union of all churches which come into consideration.

The word "community," as a translation of the Greek word *koinonia*, has the advantage of making full use of this biblical concept which is of special importance to ecumenism.[3] In Gal. 2:9 it is used specifically with reference to a decision of the apostle concerning the unity of harmoniously separated members of the early church: "They gave to me [Paul] and Barnabas the right hand of fellowship" (*koinonia*).

In our preliminary discussion, in which we bracketed the problem of practical actualization, we saw that in principle the question of the possibility of such a community of churches is to be affirmed. This is so because in the light of the New Testament understanding of charisms and of salvation history no insuperable difficulty is posed by the continuing divergences, although these are not to be ignored. The only restriction on this level which might exist is *the claim* of the Catholic Church to possess the "fullness" of the truth and the Christian means of grace.[4] However, the leading Catholic theologians K. Rahner and H. Fries have agreed (not, I assume, without support from other Catholic scholars) that "deficits" are present in every church and thus that the fullness of gifts can only first come into being through mutual supplementation by the various churches;[5] even a sentence in the outline of a speech given by Pope John Paul II points in this direction: "The Spirit of God has allowed us to recognize anew that as long as the church has not realized the fullness of its God-willed catholicity there are authentic elements of Catholicism existing outside its visible community."[6] *The claim* seems to me to have lost its edge. The result is that *in principle* there is nothing standing in the way of a unity in diversity.

But the difficulties begin as soon as a visible actualization is sought, especially with regard to structure. We have seen that even variations about which there is no intention to reach unity, that is, doctrines and institutions which we reject for ourselves or which our partners from their side reject for themselves, can be granted to the sister church within its framework. In contrast, problems arise when we adopt them (even in some weakened form attained by compromise) in order to construct a common organization.

The most recent difficulties in this regard, even though there is a readiness to make ecumenical sacrifices, have proven to be so difficult that the question has been raised as to whether we should not renounce any effort to have a comprehensive superstructure (even in a loose form). In love and respect for the divinely willed diversity perhaps we should simply be satisfied with a genuine awareness of our community and especially with visible cooperation in numerous and increasing areas of common mission. But then another question presses us: can this rather minimal actualization of unity in diversity without any structure in fact avoid the danger that human weakness will pervert the richness of the variety granted by the Holy Spirit into a hostile separation, as has been the case in the past?

It is therefore necessary to deal with three themes in this chapter:

1. The question of the *necessity* of a common organization (declarations of solidarity in individual areas of common concern, or a common superstructure?).

2. The *difficulties* of actualization in the light of previous attempts.

3. Forms of a *possible* structure of a community of churches which maintain their separate identity.

1. The Issue of the Necessity of a Common Organization (Declarations of Solidarity in Individual Areas of Common Concern, or a Superstructure?)

A visible actualization of unity in diversity is possible in two ways. The first way involves common ecumenical work in individual areas of common concern, without organization of the community of churches as such. The second way involves a particular structure. These two ways are to be clearly distinguished from each other. But even if the formation of a structure takes place, it is obvious that the first way is to be further developed within the second, organizational way—then all the more so. But so long as a superstructure does not exist, as is presently the case, or if it should be impossible to construct, then the only unity which can come into consideration is cooperative work in certain areas of common concern. I would like to note that even here everything need not simply remain as it has been, but that this cooperation should be constantly intensified and increasingly lead to particular declarations of solidarity. Whether this is the ideal state of affairs, or whether even beyond this the formation of a structure should at least be attempted, are the issues we want to examine here.

First, we need to discuss the proposals for a community of churches which would not necessarily be subordinate to a comprehensive organization.[7] To enumerate them all is not possible here. I will name only the following: ecumenical theological discussions for the production of common texts, common biblical work, common worship services, common institutes, common activities in the field of social work. I will restrict myself to the topics of common theological discussions and ecumenical worship services. In the process, I also want to emphasize that these common activities ought to actualize unity in diversity. This is not always remembered. In such activities, everyone's attention is directed only toward unity as such, not toward unity in diversity.

This danger is a particular threat to the discussions that have been carried on in common among the representatives of a large number of churches. In the previously mentioned report by Visser't Hooft, he points out that since 1967, alongside these common discussions, consultations have taken place with more and more frequency between only two confessional groups, and he rightly advocates the continuation of "multilateral" and "bilateral" dialogues alongside each other.[8] I would like to add that the bilateral cooperative work appears to be so important because, in the nature of the case, it is better suited for the preservation of the characteristic emphases of each confession in the production of common texts. But this concern should be the rule for all ecumenical discussions that have unity documents as their goal. What all have in common should be emphasized when possible, but really only when possible: that means only as far as the border beyond which there is homogenizing merger and disregard of confessional identity. This border may not be violated.

The greatest ecumenical progress in the area of theology has probably been made in the area of the critical study of the Bible. The great boom which ecumenism has experienced in our time of course had its beginnings in this area, as the ecumenical pioneer Cardinal Bea, former rector of the Pontifical Biblical Institute, always emphasized. In biblical studies the commonality is so broad that the differences which divide exegetical schools from each other no longer correspond to the differences between the confessional groups, but cut across confessional lines.[9] There are significant series of biblical commentaries being produced in common.[10]

The scholarly societies for the study of both the Old Testament and the New Testament, which regularly hold academic conferences, include specialists of all confessions.

The work on ecumenical translations of the Bible has produced positive results. We can only properly assess their value when we remind ourselves of the inner distance with which Catholics in former days spoke of the "Protestant Bible" and Protestants of the "Catholic Bible." Of course, the justifiable joy with which we speak of common translations must be somewhat reserved, in order that customs with regard to traditional translations can be respected to a certain degree in the use of these translations in this or that church, so long as such customary usages do not directly contradict the generally accepted present exegetical understanding.

Since I was a participant—though only indirectly—in the production of the French *Traduction oecuménique de la Bible* (TOB), Paris, 1975 (on its creation see the contribution of P. Prigent, "Aux origines de la Traduction oecuménique de la Bible," to *Test. oec.*, 129ff.), I mention the following indications of extensive common understanding: The work of translation was divided between Catholic and Protestant exegetes. In case no agreement could be reached on certain issues by the different translators, the decision was to be made by Père P. Benoit, for many years professor at the famous Ecole biblique et archéologique française of Jerusalem, and by me. Neither of us belonged to the group of translators. To the surprise of everyone, the exegetical agreement within the group of translators was so complete that we did not have to intervene with regard to a single New Testament passage. (See also the contribution of Père P. Benoit to *Test. oec.*, 170.)

Ratzinger, *Ratzinger Report*, 164, has reservations concerning the German ecumenical translation. On the Italian common translation, see the contribution of R. Bertalot to *Test. oec.*, 40.

With regard to common worship services, we may say first of all that services of the Word allow the community of churches to be visibly manifest without difficulty. This was Pope John Paul II's intention when he shared the pulpit with the Lutheran pastor in the small Lutheran congregation in Rome. There is today a pulpit exchange among numerous congregations. Care must certainly be taken in such cases that the basic truths which bind all Christians together are proclaimed and that no offense is provoked. But such preaching should by no means be colorless and attempt to disguise the home church of the visiting preacher in some artificial way. The liturgical framework around the sermon in a service of the Word should be so constructed that it is a sign of the commonality of all Christians, and that the traditional forms of the church in which the celebration takes place are acknowledged and respected. When a Protestant pastor preaches during a Catholic mass, that is the situation in any case.

Extending fellowship during worship to the Eucharist has of course been the subject of constant concern, but we are still a long way from seeing it actualized. This common act of worship, more so than other common activities, presupposes fundamental theological work. In the first place, this concerns the meaning of the Eucharist which, like all worship, is not a matter of mere human doing but—and primarily—is a matter of God's own activity. The Lutheran-Catholic discussion has already become quite extensive in this regard. The German document completed in 1978, *Das Herrenmahl (The Eucharist)*,[11] testifies to this, as does the "Lima document" *(BEM)*, on which theologians of many churches worked together.[12] In addition, the difficult problem of ministerial office[13] requires the preliminary theological work of multilateral debates and discussions from all concerned of the Eucharist, since according to Catholic teaching the sacrament can be dispensed only by a priest who stands in the apostolic succession guaranteed by the Catholic Church. For this reason the difficulty of the issue of intercommunion is closely related to that of the issue of the structure of the community of churches (to be discussed below).

It is agreed on both sides that the oneness of the ecclesiastical communion should find its visible expression in the communion of the Eucharist, as conversely the communion of the Eucharist presupposes the oneness of the ecclesiastical communion ("Because there is one bread, we who are many are *one* body," 1 Cor. 10:17). But the regrettable fact of the matter is that at present a general intercommunion is not possible,[14] because from the Catholic side the necessary relation to the structure of the church cannot be given up. In the Catholic Church, this is of course a question of faith.

But recently a concession has become possible. It proceeds from the fact that, after all, on other questions of faith an extensive agreement has been reached and the churches have come to live together in a fraternal relationship. So it is conceded that in certain exceptional cases there can be at least a partial unity in communion that can become visible in common eucharistic celebrations. This is of course regarded from the Protestant side only as a preliminary solution which is not yet satisfactory, and the desire for complete eucharistic fellowship has not subsided.[15]

I understand this desire. I too regard this practice of common eucharistic celebrations in exceptional cases as a preliminary solution (which in any case should be increasingly practiced). But I hope to cause no offense, and not to make a virtue of necessity, if I nonetheless find this practice to be meaningful, inasmuch as it validates the preservation of the identity of the different churches in the community: a common fellowship, and still the continuation of the practice of the Eucharist according to the different customs by which it has been celebrated in the separated churches, by which each of them brings into the foreground certain aspects of the eucharistic event with special emphasis.

Despite the consensus which has been established in the different ecumenical texts concerning the understanding of the Eucharist, I have unavoidably and repeatedly had the following experience: I perceive a very great difference in how I experience the eucharistic celebration, depending on whether I am in a German-Swiss Reformed service of the Lord's Supper, or a eucharistic service of the Lutheran, Anglican, or Orthodox churches, or in a Roman Catholic mass. (I grant that some of these experiences are more nearly alike than others.) That does not mean that I am opposed in principle to a unified eucharistic liturgy for the special cases in which intercommunion is possible *(BEM)*. To a certain degree the positive value of variety in this regard is also recognized in the Roman Catholic/Lutheran document, *The Eucharist*.

I do not want to withhold a warning concerning certain celebrations of intercommunion. I have participated in some occasions which did not entirely correspond to the requirements specified for those occasions of intercommunion permitted as exceptional cases. They do not have as their basis even a partial unity in matters of faith, but—on the bandwagon of the popular "orthopraxy"—are based on a shared indifference to matters of faith: the main thing is simply that people celebrate the Eucharist together. In such cases, the meaning of the Eucharist no longer matters at all. In view of this danger, Protestants too should avoid all such "enthusiast" ("schwärmerischen") common eucharistic celebrations. Such a "community" is worse than any separation, for it has then become a matter of "unity at any price," including the price of the meaning of the Eucharist. Such a unity is to be rejected. When it is said, with some degree of correctness, that the unity of the Christian fellowship is not only represented, but furthered,[16] by eucharistic fellowship, it is still important to be careful that the way to unity does not become a false path.

Since general intercommunion is not currently possible, I would like to return to a suggestion which I made some time ago, namely to recover one of the practices of the ancient church and reintroduce, alongside the eucharistic celebration, the ancient practice of the *agape feast* (love feast), but with the participation of the different confessions. The agape feast should of course *not be seen as a substitute* for the Eucharist itself,[17] although the early church's "breaking of bread" (Acts 2:46) took place within the framework of an actual meal. But such feasts would in any case be a practice of Christian worship which would be acceptable to all churches. What we are talking about is a full fellowship meal which is eaten together in the context of a festive worship service. The location could be in the fellowship halls of the congregations, or, even better, in private homes, alternately chosen from Protestant and Catholic families. The more detailed arrangements would have to be worked out in common. I am thinking, for example, of the way mealtimes are observed in monasteries, with silence and the reading aloud of important texts. Despite the fact that the memory of the ancient agape feasts has all but disappeared, the suggestion repeated here should not be greeted with skepticism. This is especially the case since, as I now learn, for some time now love feasts have been held in many places, and also since they continue to be observed in connection with the Orthodox program for caring for the poor, *Artoklasis* ("Breaking of Bread"), as I have learned from a brochure just published under the direction of Prof. A. Kallis of the Teaching and Research Division "Orthodoxy" of the University of Münster. I would like to ascribe an explicitly ecumenical goal[18] to such agape feasts as one of their assignments.

We have seen that in any case many forms of fruitful cooperation already exist, forms that continue to draw nearer and nearer to each other.[19] Among these we can here consider only those which have to do with theology and worship. But should we be satisfied with this kind of ecumenical activity and its gradual intensification, without incorporating it into any kind of structural framework? Many respond affirmatively to this question, and their response is precisely in the interest of the preservation of community within diversity. Their view is that the severe differences which first emerge between the confessions during the attempt to find a common superstructure will become a threat to the intended community, since it is precisely in the process of trying to find a common structure that the occasion is given for old quarrels to be revived which destroy rather than further the intended unity. This can happen especially if Protestants have an a priori anti-structure attitude and speak only of a pure spiritual community in Christ. Beyond this, a structured community is subject to the objection that it is practically the same as the founding of a new church, the very thing which we wish to avoid according to my concept, which of course foresees only a community of churches that maintain their independence, unlike the Fries-Rahner plan which provides for "partner churches" of a new united church. The objection continues that, since such misunderstandings would probably cause many congregations and church groups to refuse to participate in a structured community of churches, the result would only be new divisions.

These dangers must be taken seriously, and I myself do not a priori and in principle reject this renunciation of the effort to devise a new structure, a renunciation to which we at present must yield anyway. But is not the opposite danger even greater, namely, that a completely unstructured community is not sufficiently protected against disintegration? Is a "community" worthy of the name even possible without a minimum of structure? The question is probably to be raised all the more since, as our earlier discussion points out, a unity in diversity presupposes the acceptance of the primary truths of the faith. In this connection we have spoken of an "acceptance" into the community of churches. Without some kind of organization this would hardly be meaningful.

We have seen[20] that order as such is a New Testament charisma, the purpose of which is to protect the Spirit from distortion (God as a "God of order," 1 Cor. 14:40). In the New Testament, the spiritual gifts generate ministries within the church.

The churches, including most Protestant churches, thus possess a structure corresponding to their own distinctive features. Therefore the planned community of churches, although it is itself not a church, should also have some sort of superstructure, even if fairly loose, a superstructure which respects the churches which it unites: here too, *unity in diversity.*

Previous experience indicates that without the function of a divinely willed order which protects the Spirit from distortion, the individual declarations of ecumenical solidarity of which we have spoken execute their task of furthering community only imperfectly, or even are forgotten (as illustrated by the example of my suggestion of a reciprocal collection in the interest of Christian unity),[21] especially since they are often lacking the official approval from the ecclesiastical authorities.[22] Such individual declarations of ecumenical solidarity have not been able to prevent our present situation in which, correctly or not, one speaks of a stagnation or even of a regression of ecumenism. To be sure, the ecumenical theological commissions that have been at work especially since the last Council, have made significant achievements. But on the other hand, the documents which they have drawn up have not only from time to time evoked desirable (self-critical) discussions, but also dissension and the increase of confessional rigidity. But the truth of the matter cannot be concealed: many reactions have been dominated by an unpleasant polemical tone that is destructive of community. The commissions which prepared such declarations have, to be sure, generally been composed of important theologians, but they have often lacked a genuinely representative character, which could be given them only through some sort of structured community of all churches.

I conclude that there are dangers involved in both a structured and a nonstructured community of churches. But in balancing the pros and cons, the preference is to be given to a more or less loose structure. Some form of loose structure should in any case be attempted. This

43

structure should clearly bring to expression that in each of the churches included in the community *the one church as the body of Christ* is present, and precisely *with* and *in* their individual structures. The common superstructure should also, without by any means bringing it into the realm of divine law, still have a theological foundation.[23] But whether or not the difficulties which emerge in this process can be overcome at all is a problem which we must still examine. The only other alternative is to restrict ourselves to a community without structure and attempt to secure its continued existence as well as possible, but also to constantly increase the efforts toward solidarity.

2. The Difficulties of Actualization in the Light of Previous Attempts

Where can we find a model for a possible superstructure? Since such a superstructure must respect the structures of the different churches to be included in it, it must be created in such a way as to avoid conflicting with these structures. But here we meet a great difficulty involving an item of faith of the Catholic Church. In order to take the full range of its significance into consideration, our discussion proceeds from two matters of record:

a. Integration of the Eastern Churches

The first item is familiar from church history, and we have already mentioned it: the integration of the Eastern churches. In another respect, the Catholic Church has for a long time embraced a certain diversity. It has incorporated very different orders of monks, including those that were contending with each other. In particular, it has accepted Oriental, so-called Uniate churches, such as the Marionite. In large measure, it has permitted them to retain their characteristic features, especially their liturgical practices, but also their particular structures. They were required, however, to be integrated within the fundamental structure of the Roman Catholic Church if they wanted to be united with it.

With this large degree of readiness to make concessions to the independence of the Eastern churches, to some degree even with regard to their structure, the Catholic Church is compelled by its own teaching to include with the invitation to unity the requirement that the pope be acknowledged as the guarantor of this unity.

In principle, it could of course happen that new possibilities would arise from the most recent Catholic proposals for unity with the Orthodox churches that have remained independent. In these there is talk of a far-reaching Catholic concession, even though the structure of the papacy would be retained, but only in a very moderated form. Thus Cardinal Ratzinger writes, "Rome would have to give up its requirement that the East accept the doctrine of primacy as formulated and taught in the first millennium."[24] Here an interesting perspective for the Fries-Rahner plan is opened: on the one side, an acknowledgment by the partner churches of the Petrine service (Petrusdienst) of the Roman pope as a concrete guarantee of unity, and on the other side, the obligation of the pope to respect the independence of the partner churches (see the precise formulation of Theses IVa and IVb in Fries-Rahner).[25] For this suggestion both authors can appeal to the theoretical proposal of Ratzinger already mentioned, according to which the arrangement is granted only the Eastern churches, not the churches of the Reformation, while the authors themselves extend the arrangement—mutatis mutandis—to the Reformation churches. We will discuss below whether the Petrine service (Petrusdienst) of the Catholic Church in this form can also be combined with the structuring of the community of churches which I propose, a community in which the member churches—in contrast to the Fries-Rahner proposal for "partner churches" of a united church—remain full and complete churches in their own right. In his new book Ratzinger indicates that he is resigned to the fact that notwithstanding the Orthodox understanding of the episcopate, of apostolic succession, and of the Eucharist, which in contrast to that of the Reformation churches presents no difficulties, a complete union with the Eastern churches is not possible, since these "autokephally" [each having its own head] want to be independent from each other, and (despite the concessions already mentioned) "do not want to acknowledge" the pope "as the principle and center of unity for a universal community."[26]

We thus infer from the ancient and recent history of the efforts toward union between Rome and the Eastern churches that it is not possible for the Roman Catholic Church to consider a unity apart from the unifying bond of the papacy (at least in a modified form).[27] The same applies with regard to all non-Catholic churches.

We should nonetheless, in all candor, call the attention of our Roman Catholic brothers and sisters to the manner in which ecumenical work is made the more difficult by their obligatory binding of unity to the papacy, while on the other hand we must indicate our understanding of this situation, in the spirit and within the boundaries of the tolerance called for by the New Testament (see chap. 1). In order to express the difficulty in a simple formula, one could say: while the other churches *seek* a model for unity, the Catholic Church claims to *have* it, and to have it on the basis of and in the form of a divine commission.[28] We must be prepared to deal with this disparity, if we actually want any kind of structured ecumenical community which is not missing the Catholic Church—so important not only numerically but also historically.

We find this confirmed by the second fact which reveals even more clearly the difficulty which occupies our attention here. I mean the relationship between the Roman Catholic Church and the World Council of Churches (WCC).

b. The Roman Catholic Church's Entrance into the World Council of Churches

In regard to the model for a possible structuring of the proposed community of churches, that of the Geneva institution (the WCC) comes near to what I have in mind, as we will see, inasmuch as it does not provide for a new (unified) church, but allows each of the member churches to continue as independent churches.[29] In chapter 3 of this book I will attempt to show how my concept is nonetheless different from that of the WCC.[30] Although for practical reasons I do not approve of all the resolutions made by Geneva, nevertheless it still appears to me that, all in all, this institution provides the model for the structure we are seeking. At the same time it also instructs us in an especially impressive way through its many years of experience concerning the obstacle which stands before all efforts toward unity with the largest Christian church. This experience is derived from the development of the Geneva-Rome relationship.

As soon as the entrance of the Catholic Church as a full member of the WCC was considered, both sides saw themselves unavoidably facing the same situation which confronted the unity conversations between Rome and the Eastern churches, a situation which resulted from the claim founded in the dogma of the Roman Catholic Church that they alone can *be the guarantors* of unity.

The report composed by Visser't Hooft[31] shortly before his death concerning the relationship between the ecumenical WCC and the

Catholic Church, when it treats the last period of his account (1967–84), is dominated almost exclusively by the problem of the membership of the Catholic Church. To be sure, enormous progress in the relationship is described since the first years (1914ff.), when participation by Catholics was forbidden in the meeting of the "Faith and Order" conferences and later on the first general assemblies of the WCC in Amsterdam (1948) and Evanston (1954), to about 1958, after which time the Catholic Church sent representative observers to all important conferences.[32]

The Secretariat for Promoting Christian Unity (the first president of which was Cardinal Bea and the first secretary was the present president, Cardinal Willebrands) immediately after its founding by the Vatican in 1960 expressed the desire for closer cooperation with the WCC, and has continued effectively to advance this cooperation until today. If all the attempts for membership of the Roman Catholic Church in the WCC have so far come to naught, this is certainly not due to a lack of willingness to compromise by the advocates of ecumenism, including Pope Paul VI, who, pursuing the intention of John XXIII, furthered ecumenism to such a great extent, nor is it the fault of the present pope. It is no less the fault of the WCC, since it has been unswerving in its concern for a solution.[33] During his visit to Geneva in 1969, Paul VI could state only that the time for membership "was not ripe," since "basic studies" were still necessary—"a long and difficult way." With his sensitivity for confessional realities, he was aware of the difficulty which soon thereafter (1971) was pointed out in Addis Ababa, Ethiopia, by the Catholic theologian, now Cardinal, J. Hamer. Thus we come to the 1975 statement of the "mixed working group" founded in 1965, composed of members of the WCC and of the Vatican Secretariat for Promoting Christian Unity. This statement declares that the Catholic Church, due to its constitution, could not become a member of the WCC. Such a broad-minded person as Cardinal Willebrands thus found it necessary to confirm and renew the *non possumus* (we are not able) in a cordial letter of 1983. On the other hand, in this same writing (in which he explicitly referred to the Synod of December 1985) he again gave assurances of the readiness of the Catholic Church to continue active participation in the work of certain important agencies of the WCC, a readiness which had in fact been bearing valuable fruit for several years. He based the impossibility of full membership on the completely different structures of the two institutions.[34]

The features which he points out in this letter distinguishing the two groups are important. But I would like to reduce the hindrance to the Catholic Church's entrance into the WCC to the following formula: in distinction from all other churches the Catholic Church claims, so far as the goal of Christian unity is concerned, to be an organization parallel to the WCC, inasmuch as it itself has the responsibility for establishing the unity of the churches, and in fact, as an especially weighty consideration, it has this responsibility on the basis of a divine commission which only it has received. Whether the appeal to Matt. 16:17–19 and the Roman bishop's office of Peter based on this appeal simply raise problems rather than settling them is a matter to be examined later—when we consider the possibilities for solutions which, despite everything, still remain. But here, where we are only concerned with the difficulty of the structuring of a proposed community of churches, we are not yet ready to discuss this biblical text.[35] Here, we must proceed from the fact of the Catholic dogma.

The appeal to the pope as the guarantor of unity is the ultimate basis for all the explanations given for the refusal of the Roman Catholics to participate. This was the motivation already given for the refusal to participate in the first "Faith and Order" conference.[36] In 1916 Cardinal Gasparri responded to the invitation by saying that the pope (namely Benedict XV) was all the more interested in efforts toward unity, inasmuch as he was source and ground (*principium et causa*) of unity. A few years later, in 1919, another invitation was declined with the explanation that unity was only possible by means of a reunion with the visible head of the church. After the Lausanne assembly of "Faith and Order" in 1927, which Catholics had been forbidden in advance to attend, the encyclical *Mortalium animos* came forth, which in the most abrupt manner categorically described the only way to unity to be the return into the bosom of the Catholic Church. After participation in the first General Assembly of the WCC in Amsterdam (1948) was explicitly forbidden to Catholics, the instruction *Ecclesia catholica* appeared (1949) which, to be sure, acknowledged that the ecumenical movement was inspired by the Holy Spirit (in itself a great step forward), but at the same time warned that unity could only be achieved in the Catholic Church.

The changed ecumenical climate, especially improved since Vatican II, could not make any decisive difference in the face of this unanimity of the way unity was understood. Likewise Pope Paul VI, during his 1969 visit to Geneva, anticipated the statement mentioned above, concerning the impossibility of an entrance into the WCC in the near future, with the words at the very beginning of his address: "My name is Peter," and Pope John Paul II, during his 1984 Geneva visit, also repeated the claim that he is the guarantor of unity.[37]

Paul VI has obviously taken the unavoidability of this problem into account. (He explicitly calls it a "hindrance.")[38] This is the reason for the heartfelt pain with which he declares in *Ecclesiam suam* that "he is grieved by one idea, namely to see that he, the one who is an advocate of reconciliation, is regarded as a hindrance because of the primacy of office and jurisdiction with which Christ entrusted the apostle Peter."[39] During his Geneva visit in 1969 he added to his words "My name is Peter" the comment that "the Petrine office *(Petrusamt)*, which was created for the unity of the churches, has become its greatest hindrance." The distress caused by this unavoidable situation, which was also clear to me in my conversation with him, especially comes to expression in the words which he shared in private with the then–General Secretary of the WCC, Eugene Carson Blake, that he appears to be like someone "who sits at a great table covered with good things, but cannot eat from them."[40]

We can thus understand how it is that Visser't Hooft at the end of his report comes with resignation to the conclusion that even more fundamental discussions about the question of the entrance of the Catholic Church into the WCC would not be able to lead to any positive result, since without a radical change in the structure of the Catholic Church and, in his opinion, of the WCC as well, the problem is unresolvable.[41]

One might be inclined to draw this conclusion, *mutatis mutandis*, with regard to all other attempts toward a structural unity with the Catholic Church. In particular, we must ask ourselves whether this must not also apply to the plan which I have proposed. In view of the difficulties we have described, must we not now give an affirmative answer to the question posed at the beginning of this chapter as to whether we must not renounce any kind of structured unity, and be content with the various declarations of solidarity in individual realms and with their constant increase? If we have dwelt so much on the experiences of the WCC, it has been because we have had in view the possibility of a solution in this direction.

The difficulty can be expressed as follows: In a community in which the member churches together seek and want to form a unity, how can the Catholic Church, along with its claim to possess the guarantee of unity in the Petrine office *(Petrusamt)*, find its rightful place?

After determining and stating the difficulty, we can now answer in the sense of our earlier discussions:[42] a common structure is not possible without reciprocal concessions, *unless* we finally decide to proceed without the inclusion of the largest Christian church. A common structure would mean a concession by the non-Catholic churches in the form of a limited acceptance of constituent elements of the Catholic Church for a superstructure. It is here presupposed that a kind of limited acceptance can be found that does not violate the faith of the non-Catholic churches. And this would mean a concession by the Catholic Church in the form of an acknowledgment of that limitation of the common superstructure, an acknowledgment that could be made without giving up its dogmas.

Can the possibility of such concessions be considered at all? Is it not a priori utopian? Without being entirely too optimistic, in accord with my main theme I say: the possibility is all the greater, the more these concessions respect the characteristic features of the member churches, at least to a certain degree.

3. Forms of a Possible Structure of a Community of Separated Churches

The constitution of the Catholic Church is determined by the bond between the papacy and the council. The necessary concessions can take place in these two realms, by which the papacy always includes the council in some form or other, while the council can in principle be considered apart from the papacy—to be sure, only outside the inner-Catholic framework.

a. Petrine Office *(Petrusamt)*/Petrine Service *(Petrusdienst)*

We will at first examine—but only with regard to the proposed superstructure for a community of harmoniously separated churches—the possibility of a limited acknowledgment of the Roman pope by non-Catholic churches, an acknowledgment linked to certain conditions, as well as the fulfillment of these conditions by the Catholic Church. This possibility stands in the background of most of the models for a community of churches presented to date.

In an earlier essay on the papacy I was concerned with the question of whether the papacy could be regarded as a Catholic charism.[43] But I considered it only from the point of view of the charisms of the Catholic Church, and did not raise the other question which occupies us here, of whether this institution could be taken over for a superstructure of a community of autonomous churches, in a form that would moderate the difficulty discussed above. Nevertheless I would like to refer briefly to that article here, since it can indirectly also throw light on this second question. Previously in this book[44] I have made a distinction, oriented to the New Testament, between charism and its distortion. In applying this distinction, I have not relegated a purified Petrine office *(Petrusamt)* as such to the distortions, but—to be sure, without the appeal to divine right—to the Catholic charisms.[45] I have enumerated the different charismatic aspects of a Petrine service *(Petrusdienst)*, but each time have appended a rejection of its distortion.

Without postulating the monarchical form as necessary, I have shown that a charismatic aspect can also be present in this concentration of order in one point:[46] a stronger reaction against the thinking of the masses, to which priests and bishops are most exposed. (As an example from the Middle Ages I adduce the popes' struggles against the persecution of the Jews, which was often supported by the people and the lower clergy.) But here too the fateful distortions are to be emphasized, of which we find so many examples in the same Middle Ages.

The New Testament basis for the papacy (esp. Matt. 16:18ff.) I have reckoned among the charisms only to the extent that the saying addressed to Peter is merely or solely an example for the future, but not to the extent that it is bound up with the establishment of a definite mode of succession that establishes divine law, a subject to which we will return.

The fact that the papal office manifests at the same time charismatic aspects and distortions also comes to expression in the proposals that have often been made recently: on the one hand an acceptance of the Petrine office *(Petrusamt)* by Protestants, but on the other hand this acceptance being conditioned on the elimination of different elements. In none of the concepts which incorporate a Petrine service *(Petrusdienst)* into its structure does this office simply maintain its present form, but it is fundamentally changed in the direction of something like the older "conciliarism." [Editor's note: *Petrusdienst* normally refers to the function of the office *(amt)* to promote the unity of the church.] It is thus justifiable to speak of mutual concessions.

With regard to the following, a preliminary remark is necessary. In principle it is necessary to distinguish between ecumenical plans that have a united church composed of partner churches as their goal (e.g., Fries-Rahner), and those that grant the churches their full independence as separate bodies, but united in a community of churches. To this latter group belongs the project recommended by me and realized in the WCC. The concessions with regard to the Petrine office *(Petrusamt)* appear differently depending on whether it is a matter of one church or only a matter of the superstructure of an alliance. But since also in the first case the "partner churches" are granted a relatively great degree of autonomy,[47] which results in a giving up of certain papal functions, the boundaries are in part fluid.

In general, in the common, mostly bilateral statements that incorporate the papacy in their models (in the multilateral Lima text the question is bracketed),[48] sometimes the charismatic aspects are the more strongly emphasized, and sometimes the distortions that are to be eliminated.

I mention here first the works of the bilateral commissions in which Catholic theologians have produced common texts with Lutherans and with Anglicans.[49] In the Lutheran-Catholic "Malta Document" (1972) it is said that the papal office is not excluded, to the extent that it is subordinated to the primacy of the gospel.[50] In the text composed in America by Lutherans and Catholics (1974),[51] there is a recommendation of an office of unity *(Amt der Einheit)*, but with the condition of a reform of its structure. So too, the new Roman Catholic–Lutheran document *Facing Unity*[52] envisions a college of all bishops, with the pope as the head.[53] The "Windsor Statement" of 1981,[54] which represents the work of the Anglican–Roman Catholic discussions, goes further: the universal primacy of the bishop of Rome is explicitly acknowledged, even a certain divine right in the sense of the divine plan for the *koinonia*, but of course also limited by certain conditions.

Among Catholic theologians who are interested in ecumenism we find the same juxtaposition of the demand for acknowledgment of the pope (which for them is considered a more or less self-evident precondition), and concession to a rather thoroughgoing adjustment to ecumenical needs. We have already mentioned the suggestion submitted to the Eastern churches by Cardinal Ratzinger: within the framework of the acceptance of the papal primacy as a sign of unity, the only things required of them would be those formulated within the first millennium of the church's history.[55] In the Fries-Rahner plan for a union of the churches, the requirement for acknowledgment of the pope appears (in the highly developed Theses IVa and IVb) as a condition of the "actual possibility," although the difficulty is clearly seen ("the papacy is a still unresolved ecumenical problem").[56] But at the same time the concessions go very far (also to be accorded to the churches of the Reformation): under the presupposition of the acknowledgment of the functional primacy of the pope as a "possibility," "no explicit confession" of the dogmatic necessity of papal primacy would be required,[57] while at the same time a full consensus is to be expected in the *future* (italics mine);[58] the "infallibility" of the pope and the dogmas proclaimed by the pope ex cathedra are guarded against a maximal interpretation.[59] A thoroughgoing change in the method of selecting a pope is provided for in the Fries-Rahner plan which includes representatives of the larger "partner churches" in the electoral body, with the instruction that it is a question of a *jus humanum* (human right).[60]

Common to almost all ecumenical texts is the replacement of the phrase "Petrine office" *(Petrusamt)* by "Petrine service" *(Petrusdienst)*. Thus the difficulty described in the preceding is moderated, and one could say with Congar (after he had left no doubt from his point of view of the impossibility of a general acknowledgment of the papal office in its present form): "a Petrine office *(Petrusamt)* in the collegial and conciliar sense—why not?"[61]

The advocates of unity, especially the Lutherans, who consider one of its indispensable conditions to be the acceptance of a Petrine service *(Petrusdienst)*, appeal, not without justification, to certain statements of Martin Luther and other reformers. Thus Harding Meyer[62] declares that Luther never rejected the papacy as an institution, and always remained open to a "restructured" papacy. Over against the general opinion among both Protestants and Catholics (J. Ratzinger: "[Luther] categorically rejected the papacy")[63] inspired by Luther's harsh words ("The papacy was instituted by the devil"), the director of the Institute for Ecumenical Research, Strasbourg, France, sees in the sharp polemic of the reformer more of a protest against the individual popes as persons than against the institution itself. He points to Luther's Smalcald Articles[64] where, alongside weighty attacks, there is the statement that unity with the pope would be possible if it were presupposed that the pope understands his office not as an office *by divine right*, and to the familiar passage in Luther's commentary on Galatians: "Once this has been established, namely that God alone justifies us solely by His grace through Christ, we are willing not only to bear the pope aloft on our hands but also to kiss his feet."[65] This is already a positive stance toward the papacy as such, but Melanchthon goes significantly beyond it in his tractate on the papacy, as does Martin Bucer.[66] More recently, Meyer cites Karl Barth as an advocate of the reformed branch of Protestantism: the protest is not against the "Dass" of the papacy [its "That"], but against its "Wie" [its "How"].[67] J. J. von Allmen goes even further in declaring that according to reformed tradition a renewed papacy could be accepted.[68]

Here it seems Luther has in principle accepted the papacy, though with certain conditions. I would like to go ahead and raise here the question which I will discuss shortly, especially in regard to the citations from Luther mentioned above. Is not Luther's acceptance of a purified papacy mitigated by the fact that he considered the condition of a reform of the papacy from the Catholic side as absolutely unfulfillable, and this not only because of the individual persons who occupied the papacy, but also on material grounds, because of the Catholic basis of the institution?

In any case we have seen that there are numerous and notable voices of eminent ecumenists commending the papal ministry as the means for the unification of the church. In this connection there has been considerable shift in recent times. Still in the fifties of this century, the so-called Baumann case stirred up the feelings in Protestantism. The Lutheran pastor R. Baumann was at that time compelled to resign by the Württemberg church because he preached that Protestants should take their doctrine of the Scripture seriously, which includes Jesus' words to Peter that refer to the pope.[69] How times have changed! If the same situation existed today, denominational authorities would have to urge moderation on important Protestant theologians if they, in contrast to Baumann, were to place clear conditions on the acknowledgment of the Petrine office *(Petrusamt)*.

It is only a short step for us to provide a model for the structure we are seeking for a community of autonomous churches. One hindrance, however, stands in the way of this solution: the impossibility of the Catholic renunciation of the claim to *jus divinum* (divine right) bound up with the papacy. We thus here meet again, but in a new context and concentrated on the Petrine issue, the same difficulty which has hindered the Catholic Church from full membership in the WCC. This is why the issue of *jus divinum* is so important for me.

In many respects, it is entirely possible today to have a purification, an "evangelization," of the papacy, a transformation of the Petrine office *(Petrusamt)* into the Petrine service *(Petrusdienst)*, and this has already in part occurred. The fact that bilateral discussions are already taking place is itself already proof of this. But it seems to me impossible for the Catholics to give up this one point: in Catholicism the Petrine service *(Petrusdienst)* remains bound to the *jus divinum*. This creates problems for all outlines of a future unity which has *a church* in view. For the concept of a mere community (alliance) of churches that my proposal envisions, which claims no sort of divine dignity for itself, there would perhaps be a solution possible, as we see it. But one difficulty remains in any case. This is why I must present a brief discussion of it here in this context.

The existence of the Roman papacy, even if as a more or less conciliar Petrine service *(Petrusdienst)*, is inseparable (even in the Fries-Rahner proposal?) from an appeal to the New Testament (esp. Matt. 16:18ff.), and is bound to the episcopal office of Peter. This New Testament grounding of the claim to the *jus divinum* is not without its problems. This is not the place to discuss this exegetical and historical problem.[70] But it is certainly important for our investigation of the possibilities of a superstructure to determine that there is a problem. Thus in the following I am not discussing possible solutions, but limit myself to indicating briefly that on the one hand the referral of Matt. 16:18ff. to the pope, and on the other hand the historicity of Peter's having held the Roman episcopal office are both disputed and even denied by the majority of non-Catholic exegetes and historians.

In the first place we must remind ourselves that many New Testament scholars even dispute the idea that the words of Matt. 16:18ff. were ever spoken by Jesus at all;[71] not only many older Protestant exegetes, but in more recent times R. Bultmann and his followers, for example, have considered them to be a later addition. But even scholars who consider the words to be authentic, as I do, consider it a problem that there is nothing in the words directed to Peter about successors. This is acknowledged by the Catholic side, but the response is: if the church is to continue in history, these words could not have been limited to the person of Peter; it is not a matter of a laying of the foundation as an event which occurs only once,[72] but of a foundational function;[73] this is properly grounded in retrospect by the New Testament[74] on the basis of its later historical experiences. But neither does this explanation get rid of the problem. For here too the question remains: how is this succession to be determined? There are of course many kinds of succession. It is not evident that this succession occurs only by means of the bishop's office, especially since Peter's own episcopal office is something about which historians dispute, correctly or not.[75]

The concession made to a certain degree with regard to the way in which the apostolic succession of the episcopal office is understood shows that "succession" can also be seen as determined "primarily" in terms of content as "succession in faith," to which then the sign of the succession of the episcopal office on the basis of ordination as a guarantee of this faith is added in a merely supplementary fashion.[76] This understanding of succession as "primarily" a matter of the content of the faith could also be applied to the successors of Peter.[77] Then one would have to think with Luther of the succession of the faith of Peter (of course without his exegetical grounding in the saying of Matt. 16:18ff., for this is directed precisely to the person of Peter [but only to him]).

It is certainly the case that one can and should derive a model for an office for the unity of the church from Matt. 16:18ff. But everything beyond this remains supposition, which for some is a truth exalted above all doubt, especially for Catholic exegetes for whom a correct interpretation of the Bible is possible only in communion with the church and its tradition, but for others is disputed.

In the sense of our earlier discussions,[78] we will thus assign the New Testament basis for the papacy, which is an integral part of the understanding of the Catholic Church, to that category of teachings that a number of churches will not adopt for themselves, but that can be granted to the sister churches within their framework,[79] which does not yet say anything about its usefulness for the superstructure we are seeking for the proposed community of churches. This situation is reflected in the report of the Lutheran bishop E. Lohse, "Ökumenische Begegnung mit Papst Johannes Paul II."[80] Within the framework of his very positive evaluation he cannot avoid having to state: "(Protestant theology) can respect the ministerial office of the pope as an ordinance of human law, but it cannot acknowledge that it is established with the force of divine law."[81]

This attitude does not prevent the Protestant bishop from declaring his great respect for the pope. Could this be a pointer toward the possibility of a structure we are seeking for a community of autonomous churches?

Within the framework of the concept I am presenting here, I have already for some time been considering whether—as the leader of the community of churches to be established—the pope might not serve as its "president" with the agreement of all the churches. For the non-Catholics he would exercise this function on the basis of *jus humanum* (Matt. 16:18 would be only a model for them) and on the basis of the historical role which the papacy has played, despite many unworthy popes. For Catholics, the pope would of course remain all that the pope has meant to the Catholic Church. This solution would not be misleading, to the extent that the community of churches for which it is arranged does not have any standing as a divine institution. But there is justifiable fear that it would be rejected from both the Protestant and Catholic sides. The Catholic Church could hardly grant a Petrine office *(Petrusamt)* to such an organization, since it claims a divine legitimization for this office, while the non-Catholics see this as only a matter of human legitimization. I thus ask myself whether I would not prefer another solution—without a Petrine office *(Petrusamt)*—to this kind of solution which involves an internal dilemma. The Protestants too could probably not be entirely satisfied with this suggestion, since such a common structure would still one way or another be associated with Catholic privilege that would stand in conflict with their doctrine.

Although the question "realistic or utopian?" should not become the primary issue—and although in view of the unanticipated ecumenical progress of the last two or three decades, and also in faith in an ultimate unity, no possibility should be excluded in advance—the problem of giving up the *jus divinum* in principle is materially so closely related to the question of the possibility of its realization that this last issue cannot be avoided. Is it at all possible for the Catholic Church—independently of particular circumstances—to enter into a community of churches without giving up the foundation of its identity?

We have already touched on the question of the extent to which Luther's theoretical and hypothetical statements concerning a conditionally acceptable papacy ("Suppose . . . ") must be evaluated, in the light of the fact that he considered such prospects to be hopeless in principle. In the Smalcald Articles[82] he writes: " . . . he [the pope] would have to suffer the overthrow and destruction of his whole rule and estate, together with all his rights and pretensions. In short, he cannot do it." To be sure, the situation today is in many respects much more favorable than it was in Luther's day, as we have already mentioned, but at the same time it is much less favorable since the declarations of dogma of the Vatican I, which, so far as their substance is concerned, were only repeated by Vatican II. Ultimately it is a matter of the *jus divinum*, which is the basis of the primacy and infallibility.

Meyer sees the difficulty and does not detour around it. He emphasizes that despite everything we have a different ecumenical situation as a result of Vatican II.[83] He by no means shares the pessimism of a P. Brunner, when the latter says in view of the decrees of 1870 (and the Marian dogma) with regard to the issue of the papacy, "the open door has finally been closed,"[84] nor even less the declaration of P. Ricca that the papacy and the gospel absolutely could not be united, and his rejection of Meyer's hope for an "evangelical papacy" as entirely an illusion.[85] Vatican II, says Meyer, not entirely without justification, created a new perspective for the relations between the separated churches, and even on the particular point of the papacy. In fact, the dialogue on many subjects has been radically altered, including certain aspects which concern the papacy. But although we are not "eternally separated," to use Luther's words, it does appear to me that optimism with regard to the Catholic Church's renunciation of a claim to the papacy's being founded on a *jus divinum* is—unfortunately—not justified. It is a matter of principle that is independent of the circumstances of any particular time.

It is likewise to be feared that what is perceived to be an unjustified demand to accept the Petrine office *(Petrusamt)* in some form or other as the unifying bond of a superstructure will be met by Protestants and Orthodox with a kind of resistance that will be difficult to overcome. This resistance is—especially among Protestants—determined not only by material concerns, as is the case with the Catholic position. Of course, among Protestants too the demand to respect their articles of faith plays a legitimate role in the quest for a united structure. But on the Protestant side there is in addition a perhaps less legitimate "anti-Roman feeling" in and of itself which must be taken into account, to use the expression coined by H. U. von Balthasar.[86] In addition, one must reckon with the inability of many Protestants to free themselves from a past they have not yet overcome, especially with the regrettable tendency to allow persecution situations from past history to encourage them to continue to cultivate polemical attitudes instead of seeing them as a warning against all forms of intolerance.

Within the framework of this book we thus arrive at the conclusion that the concept of a Petrine service *(Petrusdienst)* as the unifying principle for the structure of a community of separate churches, while it does offer less difficulties than it would when applied to the proposal for one united church, nonetheless still does not offer a solution which satisfies all participants. This conclusion is difficult to avoid, although H. de Lubac—and a large number of non-Catholics share his view— takes precisely the contrasting view that the papacy is a requirement of ecumenicity.[87]

Without entirely excluding the possibility discussed here, we will thus ponder another solution that also calls for concessions, but which perhaps presents fewer problems for the independence of the bodies that would comprise the community of churches.

Only in passing do I mention that the thoroughgoing discussions of the bilateral and multilateral commissions concerning ministerial offices, although very important in themselves, do not come directly into consideration in our quest for a model for a superstructure— according to my proposal each church would preserve its own ministerial offices and its ordination quite independently of the others and no attempt for uniformity would be made. On the other hand, those considerations are very important for the proposals that have emerged from commissions that foresee one united church. But also in the Catholic-Lutheran document *Facing Unity,* the goal of which is only a *communio ecclesiarum* (a communion of churches), these considerations of ministerial office occupy a very important place. Within the framework of my conception these considerations can be valuable for other aspects, especially the question of intercommunion, but they have little bearing on the issue of a superstructure for the proposed community of churches. I am thus excluding this issue from the discussion before we focus our attention on a general council as a possibility for the structure we are seeking.

Those efforts toward a solution for the question of ministerial office move in two directions: in one direction, toward the recognition of the ministerial offices as they have previously been exercised in the separated churches, and in the other direction, toward the creation of a mutuality of ministerial offices (recently related more closely to the first direction). The Lutheran-Catholic text "The Ministry in the Church, 1981" (in *Growth in Agreement: Reports and Agreed Statements of Ecumenical Conversations at World Level*, Faith and Order Paper 108 (New York: Paulist Press; Geneva: WCC, 1984) sees the work of the Holy Spirit in the confessional differences of ministerial office. The Lima document of 1982 *(BEM)* emphasizes the importance of acknowledging the validity of ministerial offices as they have previously been exercised, but still sees the necessity of striving for an episcopal ministerial office, and commends progressive incorporation into the succession of ministerial office as it presently exists. Fries-Rahner, especially in

Thesis VII (pp. 115–21), sees the matter in a similar fashion. The most recent Catholic-Lutheran document, *Facing Unity*, 1985, develops this connection more concretely in its suggestion of a "procedural" [*prozessual*] attainment of mutuality, beginning with the acknowledgment of the validity of ministerial offices as they have been exercised previously, to be followed by a common ordination procedure for new candidates for the office of the ministry. With regard to apostolic succession, the 1981 document *"The Ministry in the Church"* of course describes succession in the content of the faith as "primary," but sees in the Catholic succession of ministerial office a symbol of unity that spans the ages and cultures. Although the document from the Lutheran side describes the Catholic understanding of succession of ministerial office as for the time being "not unrenouncable" (see Meyer, "Konsensus und Kirchengemeinschaft," 181), it finally leans more and more in the direction of its desirability and acceptance. On the whole issue, see H. Schütte, *Amt. Ordination und Sukzession im Verständnis evangelischer und katholischer Exegeten und Dogmatiker der Gegenwart und in Dokumenten ökumenischer Gespräche* (Düsseldorf: Patmos-Verlag, 1976); W. Kasper, "Zur Frage der Anerkennung der Ämter in der lutherischen Kirche," *Tübinger Quartalsschrift* 151 (1971): 97–109; and idem, "Ökumenischer Fortschritt im Amtsverständnis?" in *Amt im Widerstreit*, ed. K. Schuh (Berlin: Morus, 1973), 57–58.

b. The Council

The solution to which we now turn our attention is a council of all the member churches of the community of churches we are envisioning. In such a council there would be no "observers" as at the councils of the Catholic Church and the assemblies of the WCC—only full participating members. I note in advance: although on the one hand this council would have a great influence, on the other hand it would not claim anything like the divine dignity attributed by the Catholic Church to its councils which, like the synods of the other churches, would continue their separate parallel existence. This is because the community of churches for which this council is to provide the unifying structure would of course be a human institution, as I have already emphasized repeatedly. It could thus be asked whether, in order to avoid misunderstandings, some other term than "council" should thus be preferred, although it is difficult to think of a suitable alternative. In any case, when in the following we speak of a "council," this is done with the reservation just mentioned.

Here, we are looking at the conciliar solution independently of the papacy. In the proposed structural sketch we have examined previously, the basic component of which is the Petrine service *(Petrus-*

dienst), a council would be incorporated in some form or other. In Catholicism the Council is bound very closely to the papacy, and it is to be asked whether the Catholic Church would agree to having the council alone as the superstructure for the community of independent churches. For such a community of churches that is structured somewhat loosely and is thought of as a human organization, this possibility is a priori more likely to be realized than that of a united church, as envisioned in other plans of which we have spoken. The difficulty we encounter in this regard could at least be moderated.

But of course the difficulty persists, for it is the combination of "collegiality" with the papacy which constitutes the characteristic structure of the Catholic Church. A more precise determination of this relationship was the object of Councils in earlier centuries, as it was one of the major agenda items of Vatican II, after Vatican I (1870) was not able to complete its work on this issue due to the outbreak of the war.[88] The solution to which the last Council came is clearly formulated in the writing of H. de Lubac:[89] Peter belongs to the Twelve, but at the same time he is the guarantor of their unity; the pope, as bishop of Rome, belongs to the bishops, but at the same time he is the guarantor of their unity. Within the framework of Catholic teaching, this is a consistent combination. The Council without this bond with the papacy is inconceivable as the structure of the Catholic Church. But for the reasons mentioned above, in a superstructure common to all confessions this bond to the papacy creates a problem for non-Catholics. Of the two constitutive elements of the Catholic Church, only the Council is without any kind of difficulties, since synods are a part of the structure of practically all church bodies. Thus despite the fact that within the Catholic Church the Council is inseparable from the papacy, the question may be posed as to whether, entirely to accommodate the Catholic point of view, such a link could be envisioned as the superstructure for a community of autonomous churches.

With a different objective than the one I have envisioned above, namely as the structure for a reunification, the Eastern Orthodox churches have for a long time been calling for a general council, since they do not recognize the Councils of the second millennium, in which they have not participated.[90]

According to my conception of the matter too, we should be striving for what has rightly been called "a general, really ecumenical council." But in accord with the theological premises of my suggestion, this council would have to respect the unique characteristic features of each church. Since alongside the general council each of the member churches would continue to hold its own councils or synods as previously, according to its own rules, the Catholic Church would not have to change in any way the relationship of its own Councils with the pope, with his claim to convene them and serve as their leader.

But would not participation in such a general council over which the pope did not exclusively preside mean for the Catholic Church that it had abandoned its claim that it alone has the divine commission to guarantee the unity of the whole church? Would it not be the same situation as the entrance of the Catholic Church into the WCC? I see here only one possibility. We have spoken above of unavoidable concessions, without which we must give up the idea of a unity between the Catholic Church and all the other Christian churches. One such concession would also be absolutely essential for the conciliar solution. The Catholic Church would have to be ready to seek conditions that would allow it to participate in these general assemblies without giving up its claim. For this purpose it would be necessary to consider anew that no divine authority is claimed by or attributed to this council, and that it operates on the basis of *jus humanum*. Of course the participating members would pray in common for the presence and help of the Holy Spirit in its deliberations.

The problem would thus not be the same as the entrance of the Catholic Church into the WCC, to the extent that the mission and tasks of the envisioned council would not already be established, but would be still to be determined. In the process of delineating the mission and tasks of the council, the conditions formulated by the Catholic Church would have to be taken into consideration. Precisely this would represent the concession which non-Catholics would have to grant in the formulation and implementation of the council's rules.

I would like now to suggest a few very general guiding principles, and would be grateful for any correction or supplement.

First, how would we resolve the question of the council's presiding officer, whose task it would be to convene and lead the council? An alternating series of presidents from the different churches, among whom the pope would be counted, would not be acceptable to the Catholic Church. But a collegial presidium would not be excluded. Of course the pope himself could not belong to such a presidium on an equal basis with the others. The collegial presidium should be composed of delegates of the different churches. Their number would have to correspond to the size of the church, which would of course mean that the Catholic Church would have more delegates than any of the others. All of this, however, would have to be carefully thought through, and additional points of view would have to be taken into consideration. Here a few suggested possibilities must suffice.

It must be regarded as a fundamental principle for the deliberations and decisions of this council that its resolutions not in the least be permitted to work in a detrimental way against the resolutions made by the councils and synods of the individual churches, which would continue to be held. This would mean that, in the selection of themes to be dealt with, decisions must be made so that all the issues that belong to the province of the individual churches are excluded in advance. The criteria for this would have to be settled from case to case. Thus the separation of the charisms of the individual churches from their distortions (which we have described above[91] as an especially urgent task of the churches) need not belong to the agenda of the general council. All the same, discussions on this subject would be absolutely essential, as would contacts in general between the agencies of the general council and those of the councils of the different confessions.

Discussions concerning common texts, as well as common campaigns and projects, should also belong to the agenda of the general council, after they have been prepared by commissions that it has authorized. But it should be understood by all at the beginning that these texts should seek not only convergence, but especially unity within the continuing diversity—"reconciled diversity" is the phrase of the day. As I have noted earlier, care must be taken to avoid any trespassing on the "turf" of the member churches in which unity texts do violence to the characteristic features of individual churches. The documents composed previously could serve as the point of departure, but only after they have been critically examined from the point of view of the criterion mentioned above, and should be presented for consideration to a plenary session of the council only after review by the individual confessions. With the new council there would be a forum created within which the many different outlines could be coordinated, which would provide a better basis for the acceptance of the new texts by the congregations. The matter of the authority that would be attributed to the decisions of the general council is something that requires careful reflection. We have seen that for the Catholic Church this authority could not be the same as that of their own Councils. Nonetheless, this council would, without claiming any divine authority, still mean more than some sort of conference, especially since its resolutions would be composed under invocation of the Holy Spirit. But these resolutions need have no limiting effect on the further development of the charisms of the different churches.

The call for a council that would embrace all Christian churches is not new. Apart from that of the Eastern churches, it was sounded at the Assembly of the WCC in Uppsala in 1968 and in Nairobi in 1976. Especially Lukas Vischer has explicitly repeated it several times.[92] In the secular arena, Professor Carl-Friedrich von Weizsäcker has recently proposed a general Council of Peace. But since this would be formed only in an ad hoc fashion, it does not directly correspond to the goal pursued here of the structuring of unity in diversity through the council, but if such an ad hoc council were to take place, it could serve as a preliminary stage of the kind of council I am proposing.

This possibility of a conciliar structure, however, has previously been pondered less than that of a Petrine structure, which we have thus spent more time discussing. We have weighed the pros and cons of possible structures. We have seen that there are also difficulties posed by the structural bond of a council, but that these difficulties are not as sharp as they are for a structure based on the Petrine service (*Petrusdienst*) and that this solution is thus more likely to be acceptable to both sides and not to be rejected as utopian. Nonetheless, we have taken seriously the possibility of the adoption of a refined Petrine office (*Petrusamt*). The main thing is the achievement of a *koinonia* that is a true *unity through diversity*. However it is developed as a conciliar organization, it should, without itself being the church as the body of Christ, guarantee unity through the fact that it brings to expression and awareness that in each of the individual churches that belong to it, with its particular charisms, confessional structure, faith and life, the ONE universal church is present.

In conclusion, I would thus like to repeat the wish expressed in my prefatory remarks, but now in the light of my considered efforts: my proposal, which I dare to publish here only after many years of striving to implement ecumenism in practice, may now be examined in the above sense with regard to its New Testament foundations.

Abbé P. Conturier, revered for his work in the service of Christian unity, coined a formula for the 1935 Week of Prayer for Christian

Unity which may serve as a guide to us all: "Unity of the Church of Jesus Christ, how he wills it and when he wills it." Both are important. But at the end of this chapter I would especially like to emphasize: "HOW he wants it."

III

Relationship to Models Proposed in Recent Ecumenical Discussions

IN THIS CONCLUDING CHAPTER I will respond to the recent proposals for a realization of ecumenical unity: to Fries-Rahner, *Unity of the Churches: An Actual Possibility*; to documents of the multilateral and bilateral ecumenical commissions ("Lima" [*BEM*] and *Facing Unity*); to the ecumenical efforts of the Taizé community; to the program of the Geneva WCC; to Cardinal J. Ratzinger's *Ratzinger Report*, which of course offers no concrete plan for the establishment of unity, but contains important statements the discussion of which will contribute to the understanding of my position.

I point out in advance that I am by no means attempting to discuss the works named above in and of themselves, but that I only want to compare my concept with theirs in order to make my own intention more clear. I have in part already expressed the essential points of my response in the preceding chapters, but only sporadically. Thus what I offer here is something of a summary, in which some repetition is unavoidable.

1. Fries-Rahner, *Unity of the Churches: An Actual Possibility*

We begin with the bold plan proposed by Fries-Rahner. Although our proposals were developed entirely independently of each other, their plan is quite like mine. Like me, both authors connect unity with a respecting of the diversity of confessions,[1] so that I find myself in heart-felt agreement with much that they say in this regard. This view of unity is augmented by their remarkable understanding of the essential nature of non-Catholic, especially Protestant, churches. We are also in close agreement in calling for a community of united churches, that, despite continuing differences, acknowledges the fundamental truths contained in the oldest Christian confessions.

The point of departure, the setting of the accents, and the ultimate goal are, however, not the same in the two proposals. My point of departure is the New Testament's understanding of the diversifying work of the Holy Spirit and the charisms. My primary concern is thus to emphasize the divinely willed diversity, so that even in view of the danger of being criticized for monotonous repetition, I do not hesitate to bring this concern into the foreground of the discussion, including making the title of this book precisely "Unity *through* Diversity." I proceed from the charismatically given independence of each church, in order to attain unity through it. I do not mean to say that, for Fries-Rahner, allowing the independence of the partner churches to continue does not also cohere with the essential nature of unity. For them too, the ecumenical church should not replace the different confessional churches, which should rather "be form and expression of ecumenicity."[2] Although these clear and vigorous statements really leave no room for doubt, other passages in their book raise the question of whether the acknowledgment of confessional identity refers to a preliminary or the final situation. The latter possibility is suggested by Thesis II,[3] which affirms that "This is left to a broader consensus in the *future*."[4]

The primary difference between the concept proposed by Fries-Rahner and my own is probably to be found in the goal: they propose an entity that is, to be sure, not homogenized, but is still one united church that is composed of "partner churches," while what I propose is a community of completely autonomous churches which maintain their separate existence as churches. Although, also according to the Fries-Rahner proposal, the partner churches retain their own structures,[5] the structure of the envisioned united church receives much greater weight than would be the case in the superstructure of a community (alliance) of independent churches. In my proposal, neither from the churches of the Reformation nor from the Catholic Church would the same kind of concessions have to be asked as would be the case in the Fries-Rahner proposal, since in my proposal they would not be "partner churches" of a single church. The concessions necessary for the superstructure of a mere community of churches involve fewer difficulties, as we have seen,[6] than if it is a matter of a single united church.

The Fries-Rahner proposal has not only met with enthusiastic endorsement, it has also experienced passionate rejection, the most unjustified criticism probably being that of D. Ols in the article mentioned above in *L' Osservatore Romano*.[7] Under the rubric of the neglect of the Catholic teaching on the "hierarchy of truths," the author charges them, among other things, with propagating a positive and far-reaching radical change in the Catholic faith. Fries answers in the *Frankfurter Allgemeinen Zeitung* that he and Rahner have advocated characteristically Catholic theses, and he names "the facts of the episcopal structure, the Petrine office *(Petrusamt)*, and ordination" that were "explicitly set forth as the conditions of unity." This reference by Fries to the conditions that their outline presents to non-Catholics is quite justified, and certainly confirms the points of difference expressed above between the Fries-Rahner plan and mine.

The opposite objection is raised against the Fries-Rahner plan with great sharpness by the Protestant theologian E. Herms.[8] Fries debates with him in the Appendix to the special edition mentioned above.[9] When Herms says that contradictions continue to exist and still could be mutually accepted, and even to a certain degree when he speaks of a "constructive tension,"[10] these formulations as such could, with the necessary explanations, be brought into harmony with mine. I am also fully in agreement when he emphasizes that differences should not be obscured. In chapter 1,[11] devoted to the issue of dealing with the distortions of charisms, I have expressed my reservations with regard to the respectful silence commended by Fries-Rahner concerning obligatory dogmas of sister churches (Thesis II).

My design, however, based on the New Testament's understanding of charisma, is oriented in a completely different direction from that of Herms, who, even in those areas of doctrine where we agree, still presupposes a fundamentally different understanding of revelation as its basis. In principle, I do not exclude a striving for consensus if it is bound to a positive evaluation of diversity at the same time.[12]

But especially in the case of Herms it seems to me that the jump from his fundamental positing of differences to a "counter-suggestion" in his concluding chapter is not sufficiently motivated. Expressions such as "patience," "respectful," "amiable,"[13] are reminiscent of that kind of "irenicism," ecumenical sentimentality, which he rightly rejects. This seems to me really to be a big "jump," so that I have difficulty in grasping his recommendation of a eucharistic fellowship.

In accord with my earlier discussions of this subject, I would say that there is need here for a grounding of such a recommendation in the subject matter of the Eucharist itself.

I thus hope that Fries would not pronounce the same sharp judgment concerning my plan based on the New Testament as he does concerning Herms's proposal, namely, that a community of churches that continue their separate existence (which of course they do in my proposal)[14] would not be possible without "self-contradiction" and that in it everything would remain "as is."[15] Fries will also confirm that I, unlike Herms, do not see as the first thing "the contradictory doctrinal clash," but the mutually supplementary charisms, in the deepening of which the real fellowship becomes visible.

In another passage[16] Herms expresses the opinion that the Rahner plan represents the skillfully camouflaged plan thoroughly characteristic of Catholic ecumenical efforts since the Council, the same plan as that of the Counter-Reformation, but with other means (i.e., ecumenism), namely the plan to re-Catholicize all Christians and move them in the direction of a mass conversion to the Catholic Church. I am convinced that this Machiavellian hidden agenda exists neither in Fries-Rahner nor in other Catholic ecumenists with whom I am acquainted. But despite this I am probably less surprised by this charge than is Fries, since I have heard it—to be sure, in reference to the ecumenical proposals of other Catholics—more often from the mouths of Protestants than he has.

That such an assumption can emerge at all is probably related in part to the doctrine I have already mentioned, a doctrine propagated by many Catholic theologians and also found in many official texts (but rejected by Fries-Rahner), namely, the doctrine that the "fullness of truth" is to be found only in the Catholic Church.[17] The Catholic Church has been called a "complex of opposites" (complexio oppositorum). Into this complex—this is the fear or the assumption—Protestantism too is to be taken up. Here I permit myself to direct the question to Fries as to whether a danger of misinterpreting the book he and Rahner (now deceased) jointly published does not lie in its reference to a consensus that is to be achieved in the future,[18] and whether a clarification from him on this point could not counter this danger.

I dare to pose another question: would not the Protestant side, with some justification, be apprehensive that the Catholic "partner church," due to its charism of order and institutional organization, would after a while simply absorb the Protestant "partner church," without intending to do so, because of the lack of strong institutional consciousness within Protestantism?[19]

By raising such questions I do not wish to minimize the service which these two great Catholic theologians have rendered to the ecumenical cause. Their passion for the attainment of unity that stands behind this plan and for which they have been criticized has nothing to do with that fanatical ecumenism that we have rejected. It is to their honor that they are not prepared to settle for the disunity of Christians.

We have spent more time on Fries-Rahner than we will on the proposals to be discussed below, since on many points these other proposals are distinguished from my concept in the same way.

2. Multilateral and Bilateral Joint Texts

a. *Baptism, Eucharist and Ministry* [Lima], 1982

Among all the documents that have been composed in recent years by confessionally mixed commissions, a special importance is to be attributed to the "Lima document" on Baptism, Eucharist, and ministry (thus popularly *BEM*). This is due to the fact that with the full cooperation of the Catholic Church, representatives of all the member churches of the WCC worked on the preparation of this document, which after fifteen years of careful study was unanimously accepted in its final form by the 120 theologians of the Faith and Order Commission meeting in Lima in 1982. It has thus come forth from a so-called multilateral advisory commission.[20] In accord with the intention I am carrying out in this chapter, I am considering only those elements in this document that clarify my proposal in a positive or negative way. I am quite aware that in this manner I am not doing justice to the theological accomplishment that lies behind this document that has been circulated among all the churches for their critique. Like the Fries-Rahner plan, it has so far evoked both agreement and criticism.

One of the most important participants, Ń. A. Nissiotis, in his report "Glaubwürdige Rezeption des BEM-Dokuments auf jeder Ebene des Verständnisses, des Gottesdienstes und der Praxis in der Kirche" (*Ök. Forum*, 295ff.), reports the debate and process of reception of the document as precisely "an extremely decisive moment for the future of ecumenical relationships," and would consider it irresponsible if we did not grasp the opportunity presented by this moment (p. 319). With regard to the reactions thus far, we should here first attend to the official evaluations, of which several have already been presented. With regard to the individual reviews, it is not possible to discuss here all the articles that have already appeared. I will refer to a few at random: as one of the first publications with a commentary by M. Thurian, in *Ecumenical Perspectives on Baptism, Eucharist and Ministry*, ed. M. Thurian, Faith and Order Paper 116 (Geneva: WCC, 1983); R. Frieling et al., *Kommentar zu den Lima-Erklärungen über Taufe, Eucharistie und Amt*, Bensheimer Hefte 59 (Göttingen: Vandenhoeck & Ruprecht, 1983); R. Mehl, "Baptême, Eucharistie, Ministère," *Revue d'histoire et de philosophie religieuse* 63 (1983): 447–53; in addition, the critically well balanced article by Paolo Ricca, "BEM o il futuro dell'ecumenismo: Un parere sui documenti di Lima," *Protestantesimo* 38 (1983): 155–69, 225–43; and the polemical article by Marcus Barth, "Domande e osservazioni a proposito dei documenti de Lima su battesimo, eucharistia e ministero," *Protestantesimo* 40 (1985): 33ff. (German: *Kirchenblatt für die ref. Schweiz* [1984], 323ff.). From the French journal of Montpellier, *Etudes Théologiques et Religieuses* 58 (1983): the articles by A. Dumas, "Gratitude et questions" (145–51); J. Ansaldi, "Lima: non possumus" (153–56); L. Gagnebin, "Compromis et ambiguités" (157–60); and A. Gounelle, "Inquiétudes et refus" (161–70); 59 (1984): the article by Fr. J. Leenhardt, "Spiritualité catholique et spiritualité protestante, à-propos de Baptême—Eucharistie—Ministère"; and the theses of P. Bühler, "Baptême, Eucharistie, Ministère: Un point de vue critique," as a critical counterpart to the reviews of Fr. P.-Y. Emery and Father E. Lanne. In addition, the reports on the Lima document by A. Joos ("Introduzione al Documento," 193–228); L. Sartori ("Una risposta cattolica," 229–58); V. Fides ("Una risposta orthodossa," 259–70); and M. Thurian ("Una risposta protestante," 271–84) in *Nicolaus*. From the Orthodox Romanian side: Antonie Plâmàdealâ, "The BEM-Document in the Romanian Orthodox Theology: The Present State of the Discussions," *Romanian Orthodox Church News* (1985): 72–78; from the Lutheran side, esp. *Kerygma und Dogma* 31, no. 1 (1985), with articles that reflect critical thinking by R. Slenczka (on the whole document), "Die Konvergenzerklärungen zu Taufe, Eucharistie und Amt," 2–19; F. Beisser (on the whole document), "Thesen zur Konvergenzerklärung über 'Taufe, Eucharistie und Amt,'" 20–32; E. Volk (on the Eucharist), "Mahl des Herrn oder Mahl der Kirche?" 33–64; and E. Herms (on ministry), "Stellungnahme zum dritten Teil des Lima-Dokumentes 'Amt,'" 65–96. Just appeared: the comprehensive anthology containing contributions from Catholic, Orthodox, and Protestant theologians, mentioned already on p. 11 above and often referred to in the preceding discussions, *Ök. Forum* (Graz, 1985), with essays by M. K. Krikorian, U. Kühn, G. Limouris, N. A. Nissiotis, D. Popescu, H.-Ch. Schmidt-Lauber, R. Schulte, M. Staikos. The article just announced for *Kerygma und Dogma* (32 [1986]: 35–51) by W. Pannenberg, "Lima—pro und contra," is, as I complete this book, unfortunately, not yet available.[21]

For our purposes I can limit myself here to the goal, pursued by the Lima document, of establishing convergences. As an exclusive goal, this seems to me to represent a temptation which leads down a road that is not without its dangers, namely, that of each group conforming to the peculiar features of the other, even if this is not what the authors of the document intended and although, as Nissiotis notes in the review mentioned above, divergences are not ignored. But first I would like to repeat that in principle I consider it necessary and useful to establish the fact of convergences which are real and not forced, so long as these are really traced back to the Scripture and apostolic tradition. The foundation that is, according to my understanding, common to all member churches (the confessional statements of the New Testament and the ancient church)[22] may be expanded by modern texts, to which of course the same authority cannot be attributed as to those ancient confessional statements, especially since the authors of the Lima document, with appropriate restraint, did not want to give this document the character of an ultimately binding text.

Seen from this perspective, the intention pursued by the Lima Commission is to be greeted. But the danger mentioned above still exists due to the fact that alongside the concern for convergences there is not at the same time an emphasis on those different elements that should be left alone in their difference, *even if*, as is often the case, these differences are antithetical. Such unresolved differences should not be smoothed over, but rather emphasized, because they represent positive charismatic gifts, or simply because they must be tolerated even if they do not contribute to a consensus of understanding. In the nature of the case the exclusive concentration on convergences, despite all care, when it is thought through to the end and finally implemented, includes the tendency to dissolve the divergences in a mutual conformity. This has by no means happened throughout the Lima document, and a just evaluation of that great work is only possible if it is studied point by point with this question in mind, which of course cannot be undertaken here.

My suggestion leads in a completely different way. What I look for in the first place in the differences is not so much to discover *conver*gences as first of all to allow the *di*vergences to stand, and in them, except for the distortions mentioned in my proposal, to discover the charismatic enrichment. I am thus in this manner seeking to establish community by a process of mutual supplementation, perhaps even through obvious sharp contrasts. Divergences will remain in which we see no charism and which honesty compels us to reject for ourselves but which we may, following the example of the apostle Paul,[23] concede to our partners within their church as a matter of "weakness," but these remaining divergences will not dissolve the Christian community.

The results of such an attempt to build up the fellowship of the community not by setting aside divergences but by including them will make a less spectacular appearance than the exclusive concentration on establishing lines of convergence, but these results may provide a more solid foundation for real community than convergences alone. Against such lines of convergence many will feel compelled to protest, since sometimes one group and sometimes the other group will justifiably see in them an unbearable renunciation of convictions they cannot really give up. This is already coming to expression in the discussions of the Lima document on the Eucharist and the ministry. Many criticisms may be unjustified. But it remains the case that an undertaking concentrating on convergence and consensus, even when differences are noted, finally tends toward a fusion.[24] This is also indicated, as in the case of Fries-Rahner, in the references frequently made to a "process," in which differences are finally to be overcome—as for example with regard to the issue of episcopal succession.

b. *Facing Unity*

The previously mentioned Catholic-Lutheran document *Facing Unity*, the result of twenty years of cooperation between the Lutheran World Federation and the Vatican Secretariat for Promoting Christian Unity, in theory rejects any sort of fusion, whether in the form of previous unions achieved by Protestant churches in which their previous identity was more or less given up, or in the form of a partial yielding to a demand to return to the Catholic Church. This was already emphasized in the older Lutheran-Catholic texts (as also in the works of the Faith and Order Commission). But here the connection of the unity sought after and the preservation of diversity receives a special importance. The expression *communio ecclesiarum* used by the document *Facing Unity* I can apply, as already mentioned, to the kind of community of churches which I envision. In this connection the document comes very near to my own primary concern. But it is not able to consistently carry through this respect for diversity as it pursues the goal of advancing beyond earlier texts, in particular by reducing this diversity especially in reference to ministerial offices.

The framework for the actualization of unity proposed in *Facing Unity* is not that of the united church envisioned by Fries-Rahner, as seen already in the fact that it is a matter of a bilateral document that concerns primarily only the Lutheran and Catholic churches that are to "preserve fellowship" with each other. But the connection with the bilateral fellowship of other churches with the Catholic Church does stand within the purview of the document.

The document not only provides for a (structured) "community in ministry"[25] parallel to the community in faith and sacraments, but also places it in the forefront. Within this structured "community in ministry" the papacy would be acknowledged, though in an altered form. This plan goes much further than the superstructure considered in my proposal. This becomes especially clear in the concern mentioned above[26] for a "process" that will finally attain a common ministerial office. Here too (as in Fries-Rahner and the Lima document), in spite of everything, the preservation of independent elements is not finally decisive. The attainment of a common ministerial office is the focus of ongoing concern, and it appears as almost an indispensable structural element of the *communio ecclesiarum*, in contrast to my concept which also excludes homogenization in the area of how ministerial office is understood.

I will not here discuss the results of other bilateral conversations, such as the Anglican–Roman Catholic "Windsor Statement"; they offer no essentially new aspects with which my own project may be compared, beyond those already discussed above.[27]

3. The Ecumenical Position of the Taizé Community

In this case also I do not intend to offer an evaluation of the many aspects of the distantly related ecumenical reality "Taizé." Its ecumenical service is not here under discussion. I will limit myself to only one point which comes up for consideration, a point that was recently an item of controversy in the magazine *Catholicité évangélique*, vols. 5–7, 1985,[28] between the Neuenburg professor J.-L. Leuba and Frère P.-Y. Emery, one of the Taizé community's best theologians alongside Max Thurian. The Taizé community originated from within reformed Protestantism, and is still often regarded as a "Protestant" monastic community. But in reality, its members consciously want to go beyond *(depassement)* the confessions.[29] I certainly agree when it is explained by the representatives of Taizé that the individual confessions point beyond themselves to the *one* church. But I see in this the nobility of the separate confessions, and not an invitation to overcome them. Because the one church is present in them, they should be preserved.

In the first of the articles mentioned above, J.-L. Leuba has analyzed the causes of the discernible hardening of confessional lines over against the ecumenical movement and finds among these causes the tendencies toward a fanatical ecumenism, as I have characterized it in a similar manner (chap. 1). The author shows how, in disregard for the yet unresolved ecumenical problems, fanatical ecumenism leaps over the theological work to be done and in some unrestrained common activity anticipates a unity which does not yet in fact exist— orthopraxy instead of orthodoxy—and in ecumenical impatience, in the place of the existing confessions, from which alone unity can proceed, creates a kind of "third" confession.

It was to be expected that the Taizé community, though not named by Leuba and probably also not directly in his sights, still felt itself and its views to have been somehow struck by his article. Emery, in his moderate answer, has declared himself to be in *grosso modo* agreement with Leuba's analysis of the present situation. But on the other hand he justifies the priority of actions undertaken in common that go ahead of *(vorausgehen)* the working out of common doctrinal understandings, and (with reference to ideal mixed marriages), over against the confessions, contrasts a going beyond *(hinausgehen)* them, what might be called the overcoming and abolishing of the confessions.

In his response Leuba emphasizes anew that what is to be sought is the discovery of community *in* and not *beyond* the confessional differences. Ecumenism is not the abolition of historical confessions, but entering into a marriage with one's partner. I do not need to say which of the two positions stands nearer to my own. But I did want to bring up this controversy in this chapter, because it brings my own concern to clear expression.

4. The World Council of Churches (Geneva)

We have seen that this Geneva institution, within which all the member churches retain their independence, is the most likely candidate to provide a model for the organization of the community of churches to be founded.[30]

With regard to the determination of the mandatory acknowledgment of the fundamental truths of the faith, I of course go with Fries-Rahner further than the entrance requirements imposed by the WCC, which are limited to the confession of "Jesus Christ, God and Savior" and to praise of the Trinitarian God. A greater commonality in faith seems necessary to me. In chapter 1 on the "hierarchy of truths," I presented directives for a common view and a procedure for handling questions of faith (and differences in faith). They are necessary precisely for the preservation of the independence of the churches in the unity envisioned in my proposal, an independence which is to be respected in any case. But these directives do not stand in the foreground of the concerns of the WCC.

It appears to me, however, that the manner in which Fries-Rahner, in two passages in their book, think that they are distinguishing themselves from the WCC corresponds to reality only in part. In their foreword the authors defend themselves against the anticipated objection that their proposal is only for another form of the WCC with the statement: "We clearly demand [in contrast to Geneva] a unity of the churches in the faith."[31] In another passage in their book (at the beginning of the commentary to Thesis IVb) there is the reminder "that the other large Christian churches and communities which wish to unite with the Roman Catholic Church must recognize the Petrine office *(Petrusamt)* as an entity also binding on themselves in order to achieve a true unity of the churches, *which results in more than a World Council of Churches*" (italics mine).[32] The essential difference between the actualization of unity as envisioned by the WCC and that of Fries-Rahner does not lie primarily in the quest for a unity in faith, which in any case has always been a concern of the Faith and Order Commission, but in the fact, mentioned several times already, that the two Catholic theologians, in contrast to Geneva, have defined their goal as a united church and therefore must demand a comprehensive unity in faith along with acknowledgment of the Petrine office *(Petrusamt)*.

I mention this because we here encounter the same distinguishing mark between the WCC and Fries-Rahner as we have found to exist between the latter and myself. The contrast on this point thus relates my conception of the matter to the program of the WCC.

Likewise, the same difficulty exists with my endeavors for an acceptable, common superstructure which the WCC has met through the years in its vain attempt to obtain the entrance of the Catholic Church.[33] I believe nevertheless that my proposal would be easier to actualize—to the extent that such a superstructure for the planned community of churches is to be found at all which takes account of that difficulty. The earlier secretary, Visser't Hooft, theoretically acknowledged the necessity of a hypothetical alteration of the structure of the WCC as a prerequisite for the reception of the Catholic

Church into membership,[34] but to date it has hardly been considered, since, from the Catholic side too, hardly a step has been taken in this direction. The WCC has for the most part maintained its previous form.

Without falling into institutionalism, it seems to me that also in other connections more structure is desirable than the WCC possesses. It should be required of the individual member churches that they arouse the interest of the local congregations in ecumenism and in the problems dealt with by the WCC.[35] In contrast to the ecumenical tendency combated in this book, the local congregation often takes to heart only the preservation of its identity, while the need and struggle for unity is abandoned. Agencies which facilitate the fulfilling of this task would have to be created.

More important, however, is the organization of a closer relationship with the member churches which would facilitate a consideration of their ecumenical wishes and at the same time enlighten them on matters of ecumenical importance. In past years it has often happened that the conduct of the WCC on important practical issues has had to be criticized. I think on the one hand of the objection often raised concerning a certain politicizing of the WCC (not in the sense of a justified fulfilling of its ecumenical commission, but in transgressing of these bounds), and on the other hand of the objection of political one-sidedness. Such an uneasy feeling emerged during the otherwise encouraging Assembly in Vancouver (1983).[36]

That it already existed, however, is shown by two 1982 articles written independently of each other by two leading advocates of ecumenism and co-workers with the WCC. W. Pannenberg,[37] in the context of a discussion of unity and salvation history argues that it is necessary for the WCC to turn from its politicizing path and concentrate on its churchly and theological tasks, in order to overcome the "loss of credibility."[38] T. F. Torrance[39] points in the same direction in that he charges the WCC with being inclined "to allow its program to be dictated by the mass media," and of being eager "to use secular power structures for its spiritual goals."[40] Both authors had in view the situation at the time their articles were written. This situation may change in the future, especially since an openness to reform is now present. In any case, the spiritual renewal makes certain structures necessary. Pannenberg would like to see the central significance that the Faith and Order Commission once had, but which it has lost over the years, returned to it.[41] T. F. Torrance perceives a "restructuring of the World Council of

Churches, in which a higher leadership group composed of representatives of the world-wide fellowship of the church will be structured directly into the constitution."[42]

In the case of a general council coming into being as I have projected it, a council that would be carefully prepared for in the individual churches, an even greater sense of unanimity would be possible by means of the manifold ecumenical ideas that could be built into it, and resolutions that manifest a party spirit could be curbed.

5. Cardinal J. Ratzinger, *The Ratzinger Report* (1985)

I have already had several occasions in this study to cite Cardinal J. Ratzinger's book (1985), the result of an interview. Although it advocates a thoroughly Catholic position that I of course often do not share (among other things, see the discussion above on the problem of the Marian dogma),[43] I value its clarity and its lack of any sentimental "irenicism" and naive optimism in regard to ecumenical questions. *The cause of unity is served better when each confession presents its own doctrine as clearly as possible.* It should be acknowledged that this is the case with Ratzinger's book, whatever one may think of its contents. I can also agree with him when he points out destructive tendencies in his church that also exist in ours with the same destructive effect. I thus concur with his condemnation of a false secularization and with his description of the Protestant openness to modern thought as both an advantage and a danger, which has precisely the same sense as my discussion of the Protestant charisms and their distortion. I concur with his rejection of a fanatical ecumenism and ecumenical impatience and haste. As Paul VI often said in oral conversation, ecumenism today often means even "solidarity in disgust."[44]

Ratzinger devoted one chapter of his book to ecumenism, namely the one entitled "Brethren: But Separated." In this book I have repeatedly used the word "separated"—never in a derogatory sense—as applied to churches that are to belong to the community of churches to be founded and that will preserve their full independence. We have seen[45] that the word "separate" in itself is not to be understood a priori in a negative sense, but that in the course of history it has taken on the connotation of "separated in a hostile sense," and that separation in this sense is to be resisted. Since Vatican II, the tendency has developed to understand the word only in this negative sense and thus to avoid it. Thus the heading of the chapter under discussion ("Brethren: But Separated") is often felt to be objectionable. I can adopt this title, but would not only say "Brethren: But Separated," but would also add: "Separated: But Brethren." In this chapter of his book Ratzinger emphasizes especially the insurmountable obstacles to unity. Every ecumenical work demands, however, along with the rejection of all superficial optimism, a faith that unity can in fact actually come about, *even if* it is not justified by the observable circumstances.

The obstructions to unity correctly pointed out by Ratzinger can be reduced to his different understanding of the church, which in fact is the roadblock to every effort toward unity. This in any case is what strikes Protestants, as it did Luther, who, as Ratzinger reminds us, also challenged the infallibility of the councils. To be sure, I, and many other Protestants, could subscribe to much that the cardinal has to say concerning his concept of the church: it is not merely a sociological structure; as the body of Christ it is more than the sum total of its members; it is not our church, but Christ's; it is not ours to invent and build, but is given to us.[46]

Nevertheless, a fundamental difference in fact separates the Catholic concept of the church from the Protestant: it concerns the tension between "already fulfilled" and "not yet complete," which I have argued is basic to the New Testament understanding of salvation history in my book *Salvation in History* and even earlier in *Christ and Time*. Catholic theologians of course are fairly united in going along with me so far as this tension concerns the life we live as individual Christians. But for us Protestants this tension is also an essential part of our understanding of the church. The Catholics also of course concede that in the church the human element must be taken into consideration, since it is composed of sinful human beings. But despite this generally recognized tension between the church of Christ and its human members, there are givens in the Catholic doctrine of the church in which the tension between "already" and "not yet" is dissolved in favor of "already": in the magisterium, in the doctrine of infallibility (including in its interpretation as freedom from error in the Fries-Rahner interpretation). Here the Protestant contradiction remains: the Holy Spirit present in the church is infallible, but the human beings through whom it must work are fallible, including when they make doctrinal statements—thus the continuing tension in the doctrine. The dialogue which I carried on several years ago with Father (later Cardinal) Prof. J. Daniélou, S.J., finally came down to this issue.[47]

From my perspective I see a practically irreconcilable difference on this point, measured by human standards, and consider it to be an enormous obstacle obstructing ecumenical endeavors. But I believe that like the other difficulties it is not insurmountable if we hold to the plan developed in this book of a community of churches in which *all churches, just as they are,* can find their place.

Epilogue

Here I would like once more to express the wish which I have already emphasized several times: that my proposal not be misunderstood as a call for "everything to remain as it was."[1] To be sure, Protestants will remain Protestants, Catholics will remain Catholics, and Orthodox will remain Orthodox, but not for their own sake—for the sake of the community *(koinonia)* of all Christians willed by Christ. The community of churches envisioned by me will certainly not be a superchurch, but rather the indispensable bond that is to bring to expression the fact that precisely in each individual church *the one church*—the body of Christ—is present. Of course every church should be aware that it represents the body of Christ, but at the same time it should be aware of the fact that each of its sister churches represents this body of Christ. Wherever this awareness is present, it compels each church to form a community, a *koinonia*, with the other churches.

Three firm convictions have been my guides through all these deliberations:

1. that the strivings after unity in our time are willed by God and thus must not be allowed to slacken as though they were some passing fad, but rather must be held on to as an unconditional divine commission;

2. that the happy ecumenical achievements of the last decades are endangered not only by a kind of conservatism, and not only by disappointments, indifference, and resignation, but also and especially by a false perception of the goal engendered by an ecumenical impatience and fanatical illusion which in its zeal for homogenization goes against the stream of the diversifying work of the Holy Spirit: "variety of gifts—one Spirit;"

3. that we therefore have the duty from our theological observation post to take with complete seriousness the historical reality to which the different confessions belong, and in relation to them to take to

heart as the chief ecumenical commandment the challenge of the apostle Paul in Eph. 4:15, binding together "*Love* and striving after the *truth*." This includes respect for our sister churches' striving after the truth.

Notes

Prologue

1. Broadcast on German Swiss radio on Oct. 15, 1984. Given in French and in revised form, on Feb. 11, 1985, in the Académie des Sciences morales et politiques in Paris (see *Annuaire de l'Académie des Sciences morales et politiques* [1985]: 97ff.) and in Italian on Feb. 5, 1985, in the Waldensian Faculty in Rome (see "L'ecumenismo dell' unità nella divèrsità secondo il Nuovo Testamento," *Protestantesimo* 40 [1985]: 129–39).

2. H. Fries and K. Rahner, *Unity of the Churches: An Actual Possibility*, trans. R. Gritsch and E. Gritsch (Philadelphia: Fortress Press; New York–Ramsey, N.J.: Paulist Press, 1985). (Original German text, *Einigung der Kirchen—reale Möglichkeit?* [Freiburg, 1983].) Hereafter cited as "Fries-Rahner," although after p. 6 the commentaries to these eight theses are divided between their respective authors. In 1985 an expanded edition was published with the addition of "Zustimmung und Kritik. Eine Bilanz" [Agreement and Critique. A Balance] by Fries. Since this addition is the only change from the 1983 edition, the expanded edition of 1985 will only be referred to when this addition is cited. Hereafter the expanded edition will be referred to as "Fries."

3. Fries-Rahner has received both affirmative and critical reviews. An especially good example of the former is E. Jüngel ("Ein Schritt voran. Einigung der Kirchen als reale Möglichkeit," *Süddeutsche Zeitung* [Oct. 1–2, 1983]), who was inclined to regard the book "as the most important publication" of the year and to agree with its theses from the Protestant standpoint. Critical reviews—well represented by that of the Protestant theologian E. Herms (*Einheit der Christen in der Gemeinschaft der Kirchen. Die ökumenische Bewegung im Lichte der reformatorischen Theologie. Antwort auf den Rahnerplan* [Göttingen: Vandenhoeck & Ruprecht, 1984]), which we survey below on pp. 67–68—are discussed by H. Fries in the supplementary chapter of the expanded second edition, *Einigung der Kirchen—reale Möglichkeit* (pp. 157–89 [translator's note: this unfortunately appeared too late to be included in the English translation, *Unity of the Churches*, which was made from the 1983 edition]). Of those reviews which subsequently appeared, see esp. the critique of Prof. D. Ols, O.P., from the Angelicum in Rome in *L'Osservatore Romano* (Feb. 25–26, 1985), "Scorciatoie ecumeniche," which caused some sensation due to the location of its appearance. (See the response by H. Fries, "Im Horizont von vorgestern" [lit.: In

the Perspective of Day before Yesterday], in *Rheinischer Merkur* [March 16, 1985].) Much more balanced than Ols's article, and advancing the discussion, is that of his colleague A. Nichols, O.P., concerning Fries-Rahner ("One in Christ, Abbaye von Turvey," in *L'Osservatore Romano* [Feb. 25–26, 1985]).

4. E. Schlink, *Ökumenische Dogmatik, Grundzüge* (Göttingen: Vandenhoeck & Ruprecht, 1983). But see pp. 16, 17–18, 19, 55, 56 below.

5. A good summary appears in H. Meyer's report of the dialogue between the Roman Catholic Church and the World Lutheran Council, "Konsensus and Kirchengemeinschaft," *Kerygma und Dogma* 31 (1985): 174–200.

6. World Council of Churches (WCC), Commission on Faith and Order, *Baptism, Eucharist and Ministry*, Faith and Order Paper 111 (Geneva: WCC, 1982) (hereafter cited as *BEM*).

7. V. von Aristi, ed., *Das Papsttum. Dienst oder Hindernis für die Ökumene?* Beiträge von V. von Aristi, H. Blank, H. Fries, A. Heron, A. Kallis, W. Kasper, H. Meyer, W. Pannenberg, D. Papendreou (Regensburg: Pustet, 1985).

8. In addition to J.-L. Leuba's foundational older work, *Institution et l'événement* (Neuchâtel and Paris: Delachaux & Niestlé, 1950), see, among others, his "Ökumenische Amphiktyonie," in *Ökumene, Möglichkeiten und Grenzen heute*, Zum 80. Geburtstag von O. Cullmann, ed. K. Froehlich (Tübingen: J. C. B. Mohr [Paul Siebeck], 1982), 86ff. (cited hereafter as *Möglichkeiten*), and "Oecuménisme et confessions," *Internationale kirchliche Zeitschrift z. 70. Geburtstag K. Stalders* (1987): 96ff.

9. See the discussion with Frère P.-Y. Emery in *Catholicité évangélique (Eglise et Liturgie)* (Lausanne, 1985)—5 (Jan.): 6ff.; 6 (April): 42ff.; 7 (July): 45ff.

10. W. A. Visser't Hooft, "The Development of Relations between the Ecumenical Movement and the Roman Catholic Church from 1914 to 1984" (unpublished manuscript). The concluding chapter, which contains personal reflections concerning the most recent developments, appeared in *Ecumenical Review* 37 (1985): 336–44, under the title "WCC–Roman Catholic Relations: Some Personal Reflections." In this book I cite according to the manuscript which contains the whole work, several copies of which were distributed by the author shortly before his death.

11. Joseph Cardinal Ratzinger, *The Ratzinger Report: An Exclusive Interview on the State of the Church*, interviewed by V. Messori, trans. S. Attanasio and G. Harrison (San Francisco: Ignatius Press, 1985).

12. H. de Lubac, *Entretiens autour de Vatican II* (Paris, 1985).

13. *Ökumenische Forum. Grazer Hefte für konkrete Ökumene*, no. 8, ed. J. B. Bauer and G. Larentzakis (Graz, 1985) (cited hereafter as *Ök. Forum*).

Chapter I

1. Thus in this chapter when I say "plurality," "diversity" is also intended, and when, in chapters 2 and 3, I use "diversity" more often than "plurality," no distinction is intended. The words are used interchangeably throughout.

2. Against this fateful impatience, see also J. Ratzinger, *Ratzinger Report*, 155; earlier, Paul VI (see O. Cullmann, "Paul VI et l'oecuménisme," *Istituto Paolo VI* [Bologna, 1981], 9); also J. Medina in his contribution to *Testimonia oecumenica*, Zum 80. Geburtstag von O. Cullmann, ed. K. Froehlich (Tübingen: Refo-Druck Hans Vogler, 1982), 74 (hereafter cited as *Test. oec.*).

3. Cardinal Willebrands, at a press conference during the synod of December 1985, also emphatically resisted this false appraisal of the present situation and the disregarding of the enormous progress in the direction of ecumenical goals made in the last thirty years. N. A. Nissiotis likewise reacts against this unjustified pessimism in his article "Towards a New Ecumenical Era," *Ecumenical Review* 37 (1985): 321–35.

4. I have in mind such texts as the catechetical book edited by Professors J. Feiner and L. Vischer (*The Common Catechism: A Book on Christian Faith* [London: Search Press, 1975]), and esp. the texts composed by the various bilateral and general ecumenical commissions (see *Dokumente wachsender Übereinstimmung Sämtliche Berichte und Konsenstexte interkonfessioneller Gespräche auf Weltebene 1931–1982*, ed. H. Meyer, H. J. Urban, L. Vischer [Paderborn: Bonifacius-Druckerei; Frankfurt: Otto Lembeck, 1983]. On the Lima document of 1982, *BEM*, already mentioned, see III. 2.a, below).

Although it is not a collection of common texts, *Ökumenische Dogmatik* by Schlink presents the texts which have been the basis for many discussions between prominent theologians of the Catholic and Orthodox churches. Professor Schlink unfortunately died shortly after completing this important book.

5. One can thus hardly understand the objection raised against Christianity by an advocate of the French so-called *nouvelle philosophie* (Alain de Benoist), that it destroys individuality in favor of a mania for homogenization.

6. It is a pleasure to note that at present the prevailing models of Christian unity—each in its own way—call for diversity within unity, without, however, always basing it on the New Testament's understanding of the Holy Spirit, as we are doing here, and without always carrying it out in practice. (Two examples are Fries-Rahner, 112–13, and Meyer, "Konsensus und Kirchengemeinschaft," 195.)

7. See pp. 28–31 below.

8. The very difficult saying of Jesus in Matt. 11:12–13 about the "men of violence" who "take the kingdom of heaven by force" is probably—*in malam partem*—referring to the Zealots. See O. Cullmann, *Jesus and the Revolutionaries*, trans. G. Putnam (New York: Harper & Row, 1970).

9. Schlink (*Ökumenische Dogmatik*, 695ff.) well describes the turning away from the false view that all other churches are to be measured by one's own, as a "Copernican revolution." "We cannot regard the other Christian churches as though they orbited around our church, . . . but we must recognize that we are like planets which, along with the other Christian communities, all orbit around Christ as the sun and receive our light from him."

10. At the announcement of the convocation of Vatican II, Pope John XXIII explicitly indicated this ecumenical motivation for the reforms that were to be realized. Schlink (*Ökumenische Dogmatik*, 694) rightly places the demand for *repentance* and that of his own, not of the other churches, at the beginning of his section on "Die Erkenntnis der einen Kirche in der uneinigen Christenheit."

11. This is also well emphasized and pointedly expressed in Fries-Rahner (p. 112): unity is not an abstract entity, ". . . the elimination of confessional specificity. . . might drive those at home in the confessions into homelessness."

12. When Ols in his polemical discussion of Fries-Rahner ("Scorciatoie ecumenische"; see Prologue, n. 3) resists the idea that everything should be sacrificed to unity as the "highest good," then what I have said above could be understood as in agreement with him. But I maintain that his rebuke of Fries-Rahner in this regard is entirely unjustified.

13. This is why I am cautious with regard to the term used by Fries-Rahner (p. 54), "adaptation," which does not exclude imitation. On the other hand, what Fries-Rahner rightly says about word and sacrament (p. 109) comes under the heading of what I am calling "learning."

14. Ratzinger (*Ratzinger Report*, 156) challenges the ecumenical dialogue to "deepen" and to "purify" (not to change the Catholic faith in regard to its innermost essence).

15. In Fries-Rahner's Thesis II and the related commentary, I miss the necessity of designating as such those things which we believe to perceive as distortions. But this has to be done for the truth's sake. Silence is not adequate in the presence of distortions.

16. I explicitly emphasize the phrase "in summary fashion," for the list could very easily become a long one. This should become the subject of an interconfessional discussion.

17. Ratzinger (*Ratzinger Report*, 156) acknowledges this merit of Protestantism and also correctly sees that it contains in itself the same danger of "distortion" which I have pointed out: that of a *false* secularism which capitulates before the world, a danger which also exists for Catholicism.

18. See Y. Congar, *Tradition and the Life of the Church*, trans. A. N. Woodrow (London: Burns & Oates, 1964). On tradition in connection with the Council constitution *Dei verbum*, see de Lubac, *Entretiens*, 44, but also Schlink *Ökumenische Dogmatik*, 688ff., and the strong emphasis on the distinction between apostolic and church tradition in O. Cullmann, "The Tradition" (1953 essay), in *The Early Church* (London: SCM Press, 1956). See also my essay published many years ago on form criticism, "Die neuen Arbeiten zur Geschichte der Evangelientradition," which proceeds from the idea of the "viva vox" in the gospel tradition (German in K. Froehlich, ed., *Oscar Cullmann, Vorträge und Aufsätze, 1925–1962* [Tübingen: J. C. B. Mohr (Paul Siebeck), 1966], 41ff.; now also in the volume edited by F. Hahn, *Zur Formgeschichte in den Evangelien* [Darmstadt: Wissenschaftliche Buchgesellschaft, 1985], 312–63).

19. If the papacy is understood only as the ministry of Peter, a ministry "which is subordinated to the primacy of the gospel" (as stated in the Lutheran–Roman Catholic "Malta document" of 1972—"The Gospel and the Church" [see also chap. 2, n. 50], a description which appears in numerous texts which have been worked out by both parties (see *Papsttum und Petrusdienst*, ed. H. Stirnimann and L. Vischer [Frankfurt: Otto Lembeck, 1975]), then it too—with the reservation to be mentioned below—can be counted among the Catholic charisms. In the case of this charism as in the others, I do not recommend merely a conditional appropriation of this charisma by the other churches, as do most of the consensus texts which deal with this issue. (See O. Cullmann, "Papsttum als charismatischer Dienst," in *Papsttum heute und morgen*, ed. G. Denzler [Regensburg: Pustet, 1975], 44–47.) In chap. 2 of this book (dealing with the possibility of a practical realization) I will go into this issue more deeply (see II.3.a, esp. 56–57).

20. The intention of making up some of this deficit was the initial impetus for the founding of the Taizé community. Other places of ecumenical encounter such as "La Flatière" in France (Haute-Savoie) and Beinwil in Switzerland (Solothurn) pursue this goal. With regard to the last-named, see the contribution of A. Mettler, "Beinwil—Rastätte auf dem Weg der Einheit," in *Test. oec.* 132.

21. Published in English as "Decree on Ecumenism," in *The Documents of Vatican II in a New Definitive Translation with Commentaries and Notes by Catholic, Protestant and Orthodox Authorities*, ed. W. Abbott, trans. J. Gallagher (New York: Herder & Herder, 1966), 341–66. This translation is followed here. [Translator's note: It should be noted that the word "Catholic" in the quotation above was inserted by the order of Pope Paul; this somewhat qualifies Cullmann's statement.]

22. Ratzinger (*Ratzinger Report*, 64–65) mentions that this happened for some time in the selection of candidates for the bishop's office.

23. The *Petrine service (Petrusdienst)* is distorted to become a misuse of power.

24. Only if each church holds fast to its particular charismatic gifts in their purity can they fulfill their mission with regard to their sister churches.

25. See U. Valeske, *Hierarchia veritatum. Theologischtliche Hintergrund und mögliche Konsequenzen eines Hinweises im Ökumenismusdekret des II. Vatikanischen Konzils zum zwischenkirchlichen Gespräch* (Munich: Claudius, 1968), and O. Cullmann, "Einheit in der Vielheit im Lichte der 'Hierarchie der Wahrheiten,'" in *Glaube im Prozess: Christsein nach dem II. Vatikanum*, K. Rahner Festschrift, ed. E. Klinger and K. Wittstadt (Freiburg: Herder, 1984), 156–64. See also Schlink, *Ökumenische Dogmatik*, 697ff., and H. Meyer, "The Decree on Ecumenism," *Ecumenical Review* 37 (1985): 324.

26. This is specifically noted by Fries-Rahner (p. 36 and passim). D. Ols's rebuke ("Scorciatoie ecumeniche") of Fries-Rahner in this regard is thus not justified, especially since he does not take into consideration the hierarchy of truths.

Without going into the concept of "hierarchy," G. Larentzakis (*Ök. Forum*, 75), in keeping with his correct understanding of "diversity in unity," calls for a distinction to be made among the affirmations of faith. However, the expressions which he uses for this, "essential" and "nonessential," are inadequate terms for the distinction made within the framework of a "hierarchy of truths" between central and derived (but also important) truths.

27. See the extensive excursus on Mariology, pp. 25–26 below.

28. As we will see below (p. 31), we find among the Bohemian reformers an understanding of unity in multiplicity which corresponds completely to the one advocated here. It is thus natural that the distinction between the "essential" and "expedient" parts of the Christian message was also for them the presupposition for this understanding of ecumenism. See A. Molnár, "Das ökumenische Anliegen der böhmischen Reformatoren," in *Möglichkeiten*, 14ff. According to Fries-Rahner (p. 34), a distinction of accentuation exists also within the praxis of Catholicism.

29. See O. Cullmann, *The Earliest Christian Confessions*, trans, J. K. S. Reid (London: Lutterworth Press, 1949).

30. Alongside the Apostles' Creed and the Nicaea-Constantinople Creed, Fries-Rahner also place the Holy Scriptures, taken as a whole, in their Thesis I (pp. 13–23).

31. As I gave my original lecture, I knew Rahner's suggestion only from the *Evangelisches Monatsblatt* (Bielefeld, 1982), and from an interview in *Vie Protestante* (Lausanne, Feb. 1983). In the meantime, it has been extensively developed and commented upon in Fries-Rahner (25ff.)

32. In his contribution to *Test. oec.* (p. 56), the Basel lawyer J. G. Fuchs also emphasizes the importance of the ancient councils for the ecumenical scene.

33. For examples from early church history, see O. Cullmann, "Die ökumenische Aufgabe heute im Lichte der Kirchengeschichte," rectoral address at the University of Basel, 1968.

34. Ratzinger (*Ratzinger Report*, 117–18) attributes a positive function to such sects, if one disregards their radicality: they remind the Catholic Church of the importance of the eschatological expectation, an awareness which has been partially lost. According to Fries-Rahner (pp. 53–54), an acceptance of such sectarian groups into the united church they envision does not come into consideration.

35. See n. 34. Likewise, the parties within the Corinthian church should, as such, cease to exist. See p. 30 below.

36. This means the rejection of all "sentimental" ecumenism. See P. Mamie's contribution to *Test. oec.* (p. 216).

37. This is one of the reasons why I dedicated my book *Salvation in History* (trans. S. G. Sowers et al. [New York: Harper & Row; London: SCM Press, 1967]) to the Vatican Secretariat for Promoting Christian Unity.

See H.-G. Hermesmann, *Zeit und Heil. Oscar Cullmanns Theologie der Heilsgeschichte* (Paderborn: Bonifacius-Druckerei, 1979), as well as the articles in *Test. oec.* by C. Martini (p. 128) and E. Lanne (p. 208) concerning the ecumenical significance of salvation history.

38. This definition comes from Marc Boegner's book *The Long Road to Unity: Memories and Anticipations* (trans. R. Hague [London: William Collins Sons, 1970], 356), who uses it to characterize my understanding of salvation history.

39. Ratzinger (*Ratzinger Report*, 78), expresses himself very forcibly against the practice of playing off salvation history against metaphysics, i.e., against the view that only the acts of God, and not the divine "being," are the subject of biblical revelation. He sees here the danger of an inappropriate application of the idea of salvation history by certain advocates of so-called liberation theology in support of Marxism. But I wonder if Ratzinger's resistance to the use of this concept by Marxist theologians has not caused him to generalize too freely, without the appropriate nuances. I can hardly imagine that this evaluation represents the final judgment of so sharp a thinker on the subjects of Bible and salvation history.

40. See Cullmann, *Salvation in History,* esp. 122ff.

41. Leuba, "Oecuménisme et confessions," 100.

42. The Prague theologian A. Molnár emphasizes this in several of his thorough historical works (see also his essay in *Möglichkeiten,* 9ff).

43. Similarly Fries-Rahner (p. 108) although the fact of separation as such is more or less set aside in their plan ("partner churches" of one church).

44. Paul presents an example, of course in a completely different context.

45. See O. Cullmann, "Alle, die den Namen unseres Herrn Jesus Christus anrufen," in *Cullmann, Vorträge und Aufsätze,* ed. Froehlich, 605ff.

Chapter II

1. See p. 15 above.

2. Roman Catholic/Lutheran Joint Commission, *Facing Unity: Models, Forms and Phases of Catholic-Lutheran Church Fellowship* (Geneva: Lutheran World Federation, 1985). See III.2.b, below.

3. See F. Hauck, "koinos, ktl.," *Theological Dictionary of the New Testament* 3:789–809; and p. 15 (excursus) above.

4. See p. 21 above.

5. Fries-Rahner, 48–49.

6. This speech was given on the anniversary celebration of the Augsburg Confession in 1980. According to Fries-Rahner (p. 48), this statement, though in the draft outline, was not delivered in the oral presentation itself.

7. N. A. Nissiotis reports in his experience of the last twenty years ("Towards a New Ecumenical Era," 334) that he sees the greatest ecumenical progress to have been precisely in this area. I have of course emphasized that the present circumstances should not be considered the final goal, but that we must continue to make progress even in this area. See also J. H. Yoder, "Einfachere Einheit für Knappere Zeiten," in *Möglichkeiten,* 107ff.

8. However, in his report (see Prologue, n. 10), pp. 53–54, later on p. 85, he is less positive with regard to the bilateral consultations. On the question

of bilateral/multilateral, see M. Thurian's view with regard to the Lima document, below, III.2.a., n. 20.

9. A few years ago one could observe this with regard to the demythologizing program of R. Bultmann. On the significance of biblical exegesis for ecumenism, see, among others, the contributions to *Test. oec.* by J. Willebrands (p. 158), H. Volk (p. 102), E. Ruckstuhl (pp. 93ff.), A. J. Bronkborst (p. 108), L. Bouyer (p. 174), and M. Viot (p. 156).

10. For example, the Evangelische-Katholische Kommentare zum Neuen Testament series, edited by J. Blank, R. Schnackenburg, E. Schweizer, and U. Wilkens (Zurich: Benziger; Neukirchen-Vluyn: Neukirchen Verlag).

11. With regard to the understanding of the eucharistic sacrifice, the document *The Eucharist* (Roman Catholic/Lutheran Joint Commission, Geneva: Lutheran World Federation, 1980), by identifying the church with Christ, does not exactly appropriate the Catholic understanding as its own, because it does not exclude the possibility of misunderstanding, but it does not in principle reject the Catholic understanding. The Lima document also indicates a convergence on this point (see III.2.a, below).

12. See the text of a common liturgy produced by the Lima Commission (principally by M. Thurian) in Lima in 1982, celebrated during the Assembly in Vancouver in 1983, in *Istina* 29 (1984): 44ff. The Catholic response to it by J. Budillon, "La Liturgie de Lima," is found on pp. 22–34 of the same journal. In addition, see H. Ch. Schmidt-Lauber, "Die Lima-Liturgie als Anfrage an unsere Praxis" in *Ök. Forum* (1958): 221ff.

13. See pp. 58–60 below.

14. See the Catholic/Lutheran document, *The Eucharist;* Ratzinger (*Ratzinger Report*, 163–64): Intercommunion is impossible because of the differing concepts of the church. See also Fries-Rahner, 133–34.

15. See also the important proposal of the former bishop of Strasbourg, L. A. Elchinger, for a recripocal eucharistic "hospitality." See "Directives destinés aux fidèles du Diocèse de Strasbourg sur l'hospitalité eucharistie pour les foyers mixtes," in *Eucharistische Gastfreundschaft*, ed. R. Mumm (Kassel: Johannes-Stauda, 1973), 109–20; see also L. A. Elchinger, "Zeugnis einer Wegstrecke," in *Möglichkeiten*, 72ff.

16. See Fries-Rahner, 123–24.

17. This is strongly emphasized with reference to the New Testament passages by J.-J. von Allmen, *Celébrer le salut. Doctrine et pratique du culte chrétien* (Paris: Editions du Cerf, 1984), 184ff. While he does not reject the practice of agape feasts, he is certainly not in favor of their institutionalization.

18. I made the proposal in connection with my article "La signification de la Sainte Cène dans le christianisme primitif," *Revue d'histoire et de philosophie religieuses* 16 (1936): 1ff. (German in *Cullmann. Vorträge und Aufsätze*, ed. Froehlich, 505ff.). I am grateful to Pastor G. Schwinn (Pfalz Ecumenical Commission) for the reference to the practice of such feasts which have already been happening. See the important article by J. Hammer, R. Ziegert, and A. Ahlbrecht in *Ökumene am Ort, Blätter für ökumenische*

Basisarbeit 8–9 (1985). The brochure mentioned above, *Artoklasis* (Münster, 1985), contains, in addition to the foreword by A. Kallis, the liturgy of this Orthodox celebration in Greek text and German translation. As background for all this one might consider what A. Greiner has said in his contribution to *Test. oec.*, 60–61.

19. Yoder (in *Möglichkeiten*, 107ff.) emphasizes the importance of such realizations of ecumenicity.

20. See I.2, above, on "Ecumenism and Charisma."

21. See I.4, above, esp. pp. 29–30 (excursus).

22. In his contribution to *Möglichkeiten* ("Konkrete offizielle Schritte auf eine Einigung hin," 80ff.) K. Rahner makes the condition for genuine ecumenical progress that the church does more than make official declarations concerning "warnings and limitations," but also takes an official positive stance with regard to the declarations of solidarity.

23. R. Mehl, in his contribution to *Test. oec.* (p. 76), has called attention to the intertwining of theological and sociological elements in the quest for the best possible structure.

24. J. Ratzinger, "Die ökumenische Situation—Orthodoxie, Katholizismus, Reformation," in *Theologische Prinzipienlehre. Bausteine zur Fundamentaltheologie* (Munich: Erich Wewel, 1982), 209.

25. Fries-Rahner, 59, 83.

26. Ratzinger, *Ratzinger Report*, 161–62.

27. With regard to this aspect of the possibility of uniting with the Eastern churches, nothing was changed when, at the conclusion of the last Council in 1965, Pope Paul VI and Patriarch Athenagoras nullified the reciprocal excommunications of 1054.

28. Similarly Karl Barth, as justification for his statement on the occasion of the refusal of the Catholic Church to send observers to the Amsterdam Assembly of the WCC in 1948: It is reported that "he could not regret this absence," for the presence of the Roman Catholic Church would only have "been disturbing." "(To that refusal) we can only say: You are quite right, you do not in fact belong here, not to us." See the sharp exchange of views on this subject between Karl Barth and Jean Daniélou in *Réforme* 187 (Oct. 1948: Jean Daniélou, "Questions à Karl Barth") and *Réforme* 188 (Oct. 1948: Karl Barth, "Réponse au R. P. Daniélou"). Everything that pertains to this matter has now appeared in the publication *Karl Barth— Gesamtausgabe*, 5: *Offene Briefe 1945–1968*, ed. Dieter Koch (Zurich: Theologischer Verlag, 1984), 167ff. The polemical situation of Karl Barth is to be explained from the situation which obtained at that time. In later years, the Basel theologian did not find the presence of Catholic observers at the meetings of the WCC to be disturbing.

29. I would hope for a community of churches structured according to my proposal that would have more structural unity than that of the WCC and less than the Fries-Rahner proposal envisions. See pp. 75–77 below.

30. See III.4, below.

31. See p. 11 above.

32. The whole development is clearly set forth in the report of Visser't Hooft (see Prologue, n. 10; available to me only in the preliminary form of the manuscript sent me by the author).

33. See especially the meeting of the Central Committee in Canterbury in 1969 with the report of Lukas Vischer, and the report of the Study Commission charged with the treatment of this issue, a commission which included significant theologians such as the Orthodox professor N. A. Nissiotis and Father E. Lanne, among others.

34. See *Service d'Informations, Secrétariat pour l'Unité des chrétiens* (1983), 4:133ff. See also Nissiotis, "Towards a New Ecumenical Era," 332.

35. See below, pp. 54–57.

36. See Visser't Hooft, "Development of Relations."

37. Visser't Hooft (ibid., 78) finds his statement to be even sharper than Paul VI's "My name is Peter."

38. H. Meyer ("Ein evangeliumsgemässes Papstamt. Kritik und Forderung aus reformationischer Sicht," in *Das Papsttum*, ed. von Aristi, 65) would be inclined as a Lutheran theologian to dispute this (since, with Luther, he does not in principle reject a "restructured" papal office as an institution), but he still concedes that the pessimistic evaluation corresponds to the ecumenical reality. See pp. 53–54 and 57–58 below.

39. See Cullmann, "Paul VI et l'oecuménisme," 10.

40. Visser't Hooft, "Development of Relations," 55.

41. Ibid., 90.

42. See chap. 1.

43. Cullmann, "Papsttum als charismatischer Dienst."

44. See I.2, above, on "Ecumenism and Charisma."

45. The same applies here to all charisms: we want to learn from them, but not imitate them in our own churches.

46. H. Ott also considers this true for the realm of doctrine, under certain conditions ("Kann ein Petrusdienst in der Kirche einen Sinn haben?" *Concilium* [1975]: 292ff.), but he considers also the possibility of a positive answer for Protestantism.

H. Küng, *On Being a Christian*, trans. E. Quinn (Garden City, N.Y.: Doubleday & Co. 1976), 496, states, despite his decisive rejection of distortions, "the ministerial primacy of a single individual in the Church is not *a priori* contrary to Scripture," and on p. 500: "Perhaps the Eastern Orthodox or Protestant Christian will be able to sympathize a little with the Catholic in his conviction that something would be lacking . . . if this Petrine ministry [*Petrusdienst*] were suddenly to disappear."

But this acknowledgment, which is to be approved without further ado, does not, however, imply any approval for basing the papacy on a divine right by appealing to Matt. 16:18, and by no means excludes the acknowledgment of the charismatic aspects of the papacy, which are also to be ascribed to the Orthodox and Protestant structures, with which Küng agrees.

47. See esp. Fries-Rahner, 112–13.

48. See Nissiotis, "Towards a New Ecumenical Era," 332. So also N. A. Nissiotis, "Eine glaubwürdige Rezeption des BEM-Dokuments auf jeder Ebene des Verständisses, des Gottesdienstes und der Praxis in den Kirchen," in *Ök. Forum*, where he describes this lack as a defect in the Lima text.

49. Visser't Hooft ("Development of Relations," 83) goes too far when he, of course not altogether without justification, charges the non-Catholic members of the bilateral commission with being too concerned with politeness and diplomacy and thus not expressing loudly enough and clearly enough the reservations of non-Catholics with regard to the papacy in its present form. I would here prefer to speak of the way in which the non-Catholic conversation partners found it necessary to take pains to consider the difficult situation of their Catholic partners mentioned above.

50. In H. Meyer, *Luthertum und Katholizisimus im Gespräch, Ergebnisse und Stand der katholisch-lutherischen Gespräche in den USA und auf Weltebene* (Frankfurt: Otto Lembeck, 1973), 143ff. [The Malta Report: "Report of the Joint Lutheran/Roman Catholic Study Commission on 'The Gospel and the Church,'" *Lutheran World* 19 (1972): 259–73.]

51. "Ministry and the Church Universal. Different Attitudes towards Papal Primacy," in *Papsttum und Petrusdienst*, ed. Stirnimann and Vischer, 79ff.

52. See n. 2 above.

53. The suggestion of W. Pannenberg is to be taken to heart, that this would mean that the pope would have to take care of the concerns of the non-Catholic churches. See "Einheit der Kirche als Glaubenswirklichkeit und als ökumenisches Ziel," *Una Sancta* 30 (1975): 220–21.

54. In *The Final Report, Windsor, 1981* (Cincinnati: Forward Movement Pub.; Washington, D.C.: U.S. Catholic Conference; London: SPCK, 1982).

55. See II.2.a, above.

56. Fries-Rahner, 63.

57. Ibid., 71, of course in the sense of Thesis II (p. 25), which requires that nothing which is binding dogma in another partner church may be rejected decisively and confessionally.

58. Ibid., 25: "This is left to a broader consensus in the future."

59. Ibid., 79–82. [Editor's note: ". . . Vatican I had explained that the official doctrinal *decisions* of the pope are, *of themselves*, and not by the consent of the church, irreformable" (ibid., 81, corrected translation). Cf. Vatican I, DS3074: Romanum Pontificem, cum ex cathedra loquitor . . . ea infallibilitate pollere, qua Divinus Redemptor Ecclesiam suam in definienda doctrina de fide vel moribus instructam esse voluit; ideoque ejusmodi Romani Pontificis *definitiones ex sese*, non autem ex consensu Ecclesiae, *irreformabiles esse.*]

60. Ibid., 92.

61. Y. Congar, *Essais oecuméniques* (Paris: Le Centurion, 1984), 83. On the primacy of the pope, see J. M. Tillard, *The Bishop of Rome* (Paris: Editions du Cerf, 1982).

62. Meyer, "Ein evangeliumsgemässes Papstamt," in *Das Papsttum*, ed. von Aristi, 65ff. See also *Badische Zeitung* (July 23, 1985). On the question

of Luther and the papacy, see the extensive chapter in M. Lienhard, *Martin Luther, un temps, une vie, un message* (Paris: Labor et Fides, 1983), 429ff.

63. J. Ratzinger, "Luther and the Unity of the Churches: An Interview with Cardinal Ratzinger," *Communio* 11 (1984).

64. See *Die Bekenntnisschriften der evangelisch-lutherischen Kirche*, 3. (Göttingen: Vandenhoeck & Ruprecht, 1956), 429. See Article IV. [The Papacy] of the "Smalcald Articles" in *The Book of Concord: The Confessions of the Evangelical Lutheran Church*, ed. and trans. Theodore G. Tappert (Philadelphia: Fortress Press, 1959), 298–301, esp. 299.

65. Martin Luther, *Lecture on Galatians 1535. Chapters 1—4*, vol. 26 of *Luther's Works*, trans. and ed. J. Pelikan (St. Louis: Concordia Publishing House, 1963), 99.

66. See G. Hammann, *Entre la secte et la cité. Le projet d'Eglise du Réformateur Martin Bucer (1491-1551)* (Geneva: Labor et Fides, 1984), 291ff.

67. Karl Barth, *Church Dogmatics* 1/1, trans. G. W. Bromiley (Edinburgh: T. & T. Clark, 1975), 103.

68. J.-J. von Allmen, *La primauté de l'Eglise de Pierre et de Paul* (Paris, 1977), 40.

69. R. Baumann, *Prozess um den Papst* (Tübingen: Katzmann, 1958). The Catholic Church in an exemplary fashion kept itself out of this matter.

70. I attempted this some years ago in my book *Peter: Disciple, Apostle, Martyr: A Historical and Theological Study*, trans. F. V. Filson (Philadelphia: Westminster Press, 1953).

71. The Catholic exegete A. Vögtle does not contest their authenticity as words of Jesus, but he does dare to set them in another context (spoken by the risen Christ). See "Messiasbekenntnis und Petrusverheissung," *Biblische Zeitschrift* 1 (1957): 252–72; 2 (1958): 85–102; and "Jesus und die Kirche," in the Festschrift for O. Karrer, *Begegnung der Christen. Studien evangelischer und katholischer Theologen*, ed. M. Poesle and O. Cullmann (Stuttgart: Evangelisches Verlagswerk; Frankfurt: Josef Knecht–Carolusdruckerei, 1959), 54–81.

72. This is my explanation in *Peter* (esp. 215), where I emphasize the uniqueness of the office of apostle (i.e., an eyewitness of the resurrection who is called by the risen Christ, one who belongs to the Twelve and was called by the incarnate Christ).

73. Fries-Rahner, 64ff. Opposed by Schlink, *Ökumenische Dogmatik*, 595. He makes a good distinction between the one-time laying of the foundation, *Peter*, and the continuing building of the church, *Christ* (Matt. 16:18: "*I* will build my church").

74. As argued, for example, by the Catholic theologian W. Kasper, "Das Petrusamt in ökumenischer Perspektive," in *In der Nachfolge Jesu Christi: Zum Besuch des Papstes*, ed. K. Lehmann (Freiburg, Basel, and Vienna: Herder, 1980), 93–122. H. de Lubac cites (from memory) a statement of the Neuenburg reformed theologian J.-J. von Allmen: "the thesis about the papacy is very solid *(tres forte)* biblically."

75. I have my doubts about the answer given by G. Maffei (*Il dialogo ecumenico sulla successione attorno all' opera de Oscar Cullmann* [Rome: Libreria Editrice Salesiana, 1979]), but it is helpful that the author has grasped the problem.

76. See Fries-Rahner, 99–100. On apostolic succession of those who hold ministerial office, see pp. 59–60 (excursus) below. The primary character of the succession of the "apostolic message of the Christ" is also emphasized by Schlink, *Ökumenische Dogmatik*, 619ff.

77. That episcopal and Petrine succession are not to be separated is emphasized also by de Lubac (*Entretiens*, 53ff.), but of course not exactly in the sense of a succession limited to the content of faith. For support he cites (again from memory) von Allmen.

78. See chap. 1.

79. I continue to emphasize this in order to avoid misunderstandings of my concept. See what was said previously concerning the "weak in the faith," pp. 27–28 above.

80. Bishop E. Lohse, "Ökumenische Begegnung mit Papst Johannes Paul II," in *Möglichkeiten*, 32ff.

81. Ibid., 37.

82. *Bekenntnisschriften*, 429. I am grateful to M. Lienhard for this reference. See "Smalcald Articles," Article IV. [The Papacy], *Book of Concord*, 298–301, esp. 299.

83. Harding Meyer, "Ein evangeliumsgemässes Papstamt," in *Das Papsttum*, ed. von Aristi, 84ff. His interpretation of the decrees of 1870 is noteworthy (pp. 76ff.).

84. P. Brunner, "Reform-Reformation, Einst-Heute," *Kerygma und Dogma* 13 (1967): 182, on which see Meyer, "Ein evangeliumsgemässes Papstamt," in *Das Papsttum*, ed. von Aristi, 74–75.

85. P. Ricca, "Ende des Papsttums?" *Materialdienst des konfessionskundlichen Instituts Bensheim* 30 (1979): 106–11 (cited by Meyer, "Ein evangeliumsgemässes Papstamt," in *Das Papsttum*, ed. von Aristi, 76ff.).

86. H. U. von Balthasar, *Der antirömische Affekt* (Freiburg, Basel, and Vienna: Herder, 1974).

87. De Lubac, *Entretiens*, 68.

88. L. Vischer has provided a penetrating report on the last Council's debate related to this issue and its effects in "L'accueil réservé aux débats sur la collégialité," in *La réception de Vatican II*, ed. G. Alberigo and J.-P. Jossua (Paris: Editions du Cerf, 1985), an English version of which is published as "After the Debate on Collegiality" (*Ecumenical Review* 37 [1985]: 306–19).

89. De Lubac, *Entretiens*, 53.

90. B. de Margerie ("L'analogie dans l'oecuménicité des Conciles notion clef pour l'avenir de l'oecuménisme," *Revue Thomiste* 84 [1984]: 425–45) has made the interesting proposal for a council that would include the Eastern churches—in which the Eastern councils would be newly read and interpreted in the light of Western theology, and the Western councils in the light

of Eastern theology. This would of course at first involve only the Eastern churches, but could then be extended to the non-Catholic churches of the West. However, in the background of de Margerie's thought stands the expectation that through the council all this would finally flow into the Petrine magisterium.

G. Larentzakis (in *Ök. Forum*, 70) suggests that the last synod common to the Eastern and Western churches, that of Constantinople in 879/80, which made ecumenical decisions still important today, be acknowledged as the eighth Ecumenical Council.

91. See I.2, "Ecumenism and Charisma."

92. Most recently in Vischer's article ("After the Debate on Collegiality," 316ff.) in which he also refers to the difficulty of its realization. In any case, he rightly rejects its connection with the year 2000 suggested by North American theologians. (See his essay, "Ein heiliges Jahr?" in *Möglichkeiten*, 155ff.) Within the framework of my concept the council would have a different character, as the foundation for an ecumenical superstructure.

Chapter III

1. Fries-Rahner, esp. 112–14.

2. Ibid., 112–13.

3. Ibid., 25.

4. Ibid. (italics mine). In contrast, I have already, at the beginning of the New Testament section of this book (above, pp. 14–16), emphasized that for me the preservation of the charismatically given characteristic features of each confession is not something preliminary, but a part of the ultimate goal.

5. Fries-Rahner, 45, 50–51.

6. See II.3, "Forms of a Possible Structure of a Community of Separated Churches," throughout.

7. See Prologue, n. 3; Visser't Hooft ("Development of Relations," 87) rejects Ols's article, but as he says, he can still understand that Catholics cannot accept the Fries-Rahner proposal.

8. Herms, *Einheit der Christen.*

9. Fries, "Zustimmung und Kritik. Eine Bilanz" (Agreement and Critique. A Balance), 178ff.

10. Herms, *Einheit der Christen*, 189.

11. See pp. 18–19 above; also pp. 27–28 (excursus).

12. See pp. 71–72 below.

13. Herms, *Einheit der Christen*, 88, 89.

14. On the word "separate," see pp. 77–78 below and pp. 31–32 above.

15. Fries (pp. 188–89): "A confirmation of the prior status quo." With regard to my position on this, see the conclusion of chap. 1 (pp. 32–33), and the Epilogue (pp. 81–82) as well as what was said on p. 14 above in response to Y. Congar's remark on this subject. See also Meyer, "Konsensus und Kirchengemeinschaft," who sharply rejects Herms's thesis (esp. p. 188 n. 48).

16. E. Herms, "Ökumene im Zeichen der Glaubensfreieit," *Una Sancta* (1984): 193, but also in *Einheit der Christen*, 47 and passim.

17. See pp. 24–25, 36 above.

18. See pp. 14, 52–53 above.

19. This is only partially a charismatic trait. See p. 20 above.

20. *Baptism, Eucharist and Ministry*, Faith and Order Paper 111 (Geneva: WCC, 1982). Max Thurian ("Una risposta protestante," *Nicolaus. Rivista de Teologia ecumenico-patristica*, Anno XI, fasc. 1 [Bari: Istituto di Teologia ecumenico-patristica, 1983], 276ff.) has shown that the objection raised against multilateral documents of seeking the "least common denominator" is unjustified, if only because multilateral texts are always at the same time bilateral. On the question "multilateral-bilateral," see p. 38 above.

21. [Editor's note: This is now published: "Lima—pro und contra," *Kerygma und Dogma* 32 (1986): 35–51. See also the treatment of *BEM* by John Reumann in *The Supper of the Lord: The New Testament, Ecumenical Dialogues, and Faith and Order on Eucharist* (Philadelphia: Fortress Press, 1985), 137–77. One should also consult the WCC's Faith and Order Papers published subsequent to *BEM*.]

22. See pp. 23–25 above.

23. See pp. 26–28 above.

24. A. Dumas ("L'oecuménisme selon O. Cullmann," *Réforme* [Feb. 1985]) considers the suggestion made in my lecture in the Pariser Institut de France (see Prologue, n. 1, above) to be "more fundamental and more realistic than the convergence document (Lima), since it would risk the homogenization of our differences in order finally to attain to unity." See also Dumas, "Gratitude et questions."

25. See the critical discussion of the document on this point by B. Brenner ("Verkirchlichung der Ökumene vor uns?" *Deutsches Pfarrerblatt* 85 [1985]: 424–25).

26. See pp. 59–60 above.

27. This is the case, for example, with regard to the texts that have emerged from the bilateral deliberations of the Orthodox and Roman Catholic churches (1980 Patmos, Rhodes; 1982 Munich; 1984 Crete), and from the conversations between the Orthodox and Anglican churches (Dublin 1984). (The latter distinguishes sharply between agreement and points of divergence.) Of recent discussions between churches which originated in the Reformation: see that between the Anglicans and Lutherans in the USA, 1980 (on which see R. H. Fuller, "Sukzession oder Ordination," in *Möglichkeiten*, 24ff.).

28. See p. 11 above.

29. Frère P.-Y. Emery has clearly developed this standpoint in his contribution, "Fur eine ökumenische 'Prospektive,'" in *Möglichkeiten*, 96ff.

30. This still applies, so far as the structural model is concerned, even though the WCC at its assembly in Nairobi and also later emphasized that it is not a federation, but a "conciliar fellowship" of churches. *Istina* (1976): 225ff.; see also "Quatre questions posées à Vancouver," *Istina* 29 (1984):4.

31. Fries-Rahner, 6.

32. Ibid., 83.

33. See II.2.b, above.

34. See p. 49 above.

35. A. Birmele ("Le travail oecuménique au niveau local," in *Test. oec.*, 42–43; more extensively in "Les efforts oecuméniques au niveau local," *Cahiers de l'Association des Pasteurs de France* 16 [1985]: 14ff.) expresses a similar view, without regard to the WCC.

36. See the report by B. Dupuy ("La tente et le camp: Les deux dimensions de l'Assemblée de Vancouver," *Istina* 29 [1984]: 10ff.).

37. Pannenberg, "Eine geistliche Erneuerung der Ökumene," in *Möglichkeiten*, 112ff.

38. Ibid., 122.

39. T. F. Torrance, "Ökumene und Rom," in *Möglichkeiten*, 40ff.

40. Ibid., 44. The patriarch of Constantinople, Demetrius I, had already, on the occasion of the celebration of the twenty-fifth anniversary of the WCC, warned of a crisis which would "shake the foundations of the ecumenical movement and the ecumenical Council." He protested against "a more or less one-sided turning of the ecumenical Council toward sociopolitical goals" (cited by M. Staikos, *Ök. Forum*, 195, in his article on the Lima text, in which he expresses the opinion that the WCC had made a detour from its true mission, for which it had been reproved, but now a return to the right track can be perceived).

41. Pannenberg, "Eine geistliche Erneuerung der Ökumene," in *Möglichkeiten*, 122–23; also see idem, "Die Arbeit von Faith and Order im Kontext der ökumenischen Bewegung," *Ökumenische Rundschau* 31 (1982): 47ff.

42. Torrance, "Ökumene und Rom," in *Möglichkeiten*, 44.

43. See pp. 25–26 (excursus) above.

44. "Solidarité dans la souffrance" [translator's note: The French expression is more amenable to translation as "solidarity in suspense" than is the German expression translated in the text above]. One of the primary objections raised against Ratzinger's book from the Catholic side concerns its pessimistic evaluation of the present situation. De Lubac (*Entretiens*, 113ff.) sees rather the positive factor in this alleged pessimism: the implied appeal to eliminate the present deplorable state of affairs.

45. See pp. 30–31 above.

46. Ratzinger, *Ratzinger Report*, 48ff. As for the rest, he strongly resists the exclusiveness with which the church since Vatican II has been described with the Old Testament concept of the "people of God," while the New Testament idea of the "body of Christ" is forgotten. De Lubac (*Entretiens*, 42ff.) emphasizes in conjunction with the encyclical *De Mystici corporis* and the constitution of the Council, *Lumen gentium*, that the two concepts are complementary.

47. O. Cullmann, "Ecriture et Tradition," in the journal which has since been discontinued, *Dieu vivant* 23 (1953): 45–67, and Daniélou's response, "Résponse à Oscar Cullmann," *Dieu vivant* 24 (1953): 105–16; see also the contribution by F. Christ, "Oscar Cullmann und Jean Daniélou im Gespräch," in *Test. oec.*, 110.

Epilogue

1. The title which Gérard Soulages uses for the bulletin published by him and for the program pursued by his group, of course in a general sense, "Fidélité et Ouverture [Faithfulness and Openness]," I could adopt as the description of the ecumenical conception advocated in this book.

Bibliography

von Allmen, Jean-Jacques. *Celébrer le salut. Doctrine et pratique du culte chrétien.* Paris: Editions du Cerf, 1984.

————. *La Primauté de L'Eglise de Pierre et de Paul.* Paris, 1977.

Anglican–Roman Catholic Commission. *The Final Report, Windsor, 1981.* Cincinnati: Forward Movement; Washington, D.C.: U.S. Catholic Conference; London: SPCK, 1982 (German: in *Herder Correspondenz* [1982]: 288ff.).

Ansaldi, Jean. "Lima: non possumus," *Etudes Théologiques et Religieuses* 58 (1983): 153–56.

von Aristi, Vasilios, ed. *Das Papsttum. Dienst oder Hindernis für die Ökumene?* Beiträge von V. von Aristi, J. Blank, H. Fries, A. Heron, A. Kallis, W. Kasper, H. Meyer, W. Pannenberg, D. Papendreou. Regensburg: Pustet, 1985.

von Balthasar, Hans Urs. *Der antirömische Affekt.* Freiberg, Basel, and Vienna: Herder, 1974.

Baptism, Eucharist and Ministry. Faith and Order Paper 111. Geneva: World Council of Churches (WCC), 1982 (abbrev.: *BEM*).

Barth, Karl. *Church Dogmatics,* 1/1. Translated by G. W. Bromiley. Edinburgh: T. & T. Clark, 1975.

————. "Réponse au R. P. Daniélou." *Réforme* 188 (1948): 2 (In *Karl-Barth—Gesamtausgabe,* 5: *Offene Briefe 1945-1968,* ed. Dieter Koch, 167–75. Zurich: Theologischer Verlag, 1984).

Barth, Markus. "Domande e osservazioni a proposito dei documenti di Lima su battesimo, eucharistia e ministerio." *Protestantesimo* (1985): 33ff. (German: *Kirchenblatt für die ref. Schweiz,* 1984.)

Bauer, Johannes B., and G. Larentzakis, eds. *Ökumenisches Forum. Grazer Hefte für konkrete Ökumene.* No. 8. Graz, 1985 (abbrev.: *Ök. Forum*).

Baumann, R. *Prozess um den Papst.* Tübingen: Katzmann, 1958.

Beisser, Friedrich. "Thesen zur Konvergenzerklärung über 'Taufe, Eucharistie und Amt.'" *Kerygma und Dogma* 31 (1985): 20–32.

Die Bekenntnisschriften der evangelisch-lutherischen Kirche 3. Göttingen: Vandenhoeck & Ruprecht, 1956.

Birmele, A. "Les efforts oecuméniques au niveau local." *Cahiers de l'Association des Pasteurs de France* 16 (1985): 14ff.

Boegner, Marc. *The Long Road to Unity: Memories and Anticipations.* Translated by René Hague. London: William Collins Sons, 1970.

Brenner, Beatus. "Verkirchlichung der Ökumene vor uns?" *Deutsches Pfarrerblatt* 85 (1985): 424–25.

Brunner, Peter. "Reform-Reformation, Einst-Heute." *Kerygma und Dogma* 13 (1967): 159–83.

Budillon, Jean. "La Liturgie de Lima." *Istina* 29 (1984): 22–34.

Bühler, Pierre. "Baptême, Eucharistie, Ministère: Un point de vue critique." *Etudes Théologiques et Religieuses* 59 (1984): 529–35.

Congar, Yves. *Essais oecuméniques*. Paris: Le Centurion, 1984.

———. *Die ökumenische Aufgabe heute im Lichte der Kirchengeschichte*. Basel, 1968.

———. *Tradition and the Life of the Church*. Translated by A. N. Woodrow. London: Burns & Oates, 1964.

Cullmann, Oscar. *Christ and Time: The Primitive Christian Conception of Time and History*. Translated by Floyd V. Filson. 2d ed. Philadelphia: Westminster Press, 1950.

———. *The Earliest Christian Confessions*. Translated by J. K. S. Reid. London: Lutterworth Press, 1949.

———. "Ecriture et Tradition." *Dieu vivant* 23 (1953): 45–67.

———. "Einheit in der Vielheit im Lichte der 'Hierarchie der Wahrheiten.'" In *Glaube im Prozess: Christsein nach dem II. Vatikanum*. K. Rahner Festschrift, edited by Elmar Klinger and Klaus Wittstadt, 156–64. Freiburg: Herder, 1984.

———. *Jesus and the Revolutionaries*. Translated by Gareth Putnam. New York: Harper & Row, 1970.

———. *Message to Catholics and Protestants*. Translated by Joseph A. Burgess. Grand Rapids: Wm. B. Eerdmans, 1959 (German: *Katholiken und Protestanten. Ein Vorschlag zur Verwirklichung christlicher Solidarität* [Basel, 1958]).

———. "Die neuen Arbeiten zur Geschichte der Evangelientradition." In *Zur Formgeschichte in den Evangelien*, edited by Ferdinand Hahn, 312–63. Darmstadt: Wissenschaftliche Buchgesellschaft, 1985.

———. "Die ökumenische Aufgabe heute im Lichte der Kirchengeschichte." Rectoral address, University of Basel, 1968.

———. "Ökumenismus der Einheit in der Vielheit nach dem Neuen Testament." Broadcast on German Swiss radio on Oct. 15, 1984 (in revised form and in French: in *Annuaire de l'Academie des Sciences morales et politiques* [1985]: 97ff.; in Italian: in *Protestantesimo* 40 [1985]: 129–39).

———. "Papsttum als charismaticher Dienst." In *Papsttum heute und morgen*, edited by Georg Denzler, 44–47. Regensburg: Pustet, 1975.

———. "Paul VI et l'oecuménisme." *Istituto Paolo VI* (Bologna, 1981): 9ff.

———. *Peter: Disciple, Apostle, Martyr; A Historical and Theological Study*. Translated by Floyd V. Filson. Philadelphia: Westminster Press, 1953.

———. *Salvation in History*. Translated by Sidney G. Sowers et al. New York: Harper & Row; London: SCM Press, 1967.

———. "La signification de la Sainte Cène dans le christianisme primitif." *Revue d'histoire et de philosophie religieuses* 16 (1936): 1–22.

———. "The Tradition." In *The Early Church*, edited by A. J. B. Higgins, 59–99. London: SCM Press, 1956.

Daniélou, Jean. "Questions à Karl Barth." *Réforme* 187 (1948): 2.

———. "Réponse à Oscar Cullmann." *Dieu vivant* 24 (1953): 105–16.

"Decree on Ecumenism" ["Unitatis Redintegratio"]. The Ecumenical Council, 1963–1965 [Vatican II]. In *The Documents of Vatican II in a New Definitive Translation with Commentaries and Notes by Catholic, Protestant and Orthodox Authorities*, edited by Walter M. Abbott, translated by Joseph Gallagher, 341–66. New York: Herder & Herder, 1966.

Dumas, André. "Gratitude et questions." *Etudes Théologiques et Religieuses* 58 (1983): 145–51.

———. "L'oecuménisme selon Oscar Cullmann." *Réforme* (Feb. 1985).

Duprey, Pierre. "La communion ecclesiale." Kongress der Société internationale de Droit canonique oriental, Geneva, Sept. 16, 1985.

Dupuy, Bernard. "La tente et la camp: Les deux dimensions de l'Assemblée de Vancouver." *Istina* 29 (1984): 6–16.

Ecumenical Perspectives on Baptism, Eucharist and Ministry. Edited by Max Thurian. Faith and Order Paper 116. Geneva: WCC, 1983.

Elchinger, Leon Arthur. "Directives destinés aux fidèles du Diocèse de Strasbourg sur l'hospitalité eucharistique pour les foyers mixtes." In *Eucharistische Gastfreundschaft*, edited by Reinhard Mumm, 109–20. Kassel: Johannes-Stauda, 1973.

Emery, P.-Y. *Catholicité évangélique (Eglise et Liturgie)* 6 (Lausanne, Apr. 1985): 42ff.

The Eucharist. Roman Catholic/Lutheran Joint Commission. Geneva: Lutheran World Federation, 1980 (German: *Das Herrenmahl [1978]*. Paderborn: Bonifacius-Druckerei; Frankfurt: Otto Lembeck, 1979).

Facing Unity: Models, Forms and Phases of Catholic-Lutheran Church Fellowship. Roman Catholic/Lutheran Joint Commission. Geneva: Lutheran World Federation, 1985 (German: *Einheit vor Uns. Modelle, Formen und Phasen katholisch/lutherischer Kirchengemeinschaft*. Paderborn: Bonifacius-Druckerei; Frankfurt: Otto Lembeck, 1985).

Feiner, Johannes, and Lukas Vischer, eds. *The Common Catechism: A Book on Christian Faith*. London: Search Press, 1975.

Fidas, Vlassios. "Una risposta orthodossa." In *Nicolaus. Rivista di Teologia ecumenico-patristica*, 259–70. Anno XI., Fasc. 1. Bari: Istituto di Teologia ecumenico-patristica, 1983.

Frieling, Reinhard, et al. *Kommentar zu den Lima-Erklärungen uber Taufe Eucharistie und Amt*. Bensheimer Hefte 59. Göttingen: Vandenhoeck & Ruprecht, 1983.

Fries, Heinrich. "Im Horizont von vorgestern." *Rheinischer Merkur* (Mar. 16, 1985).

———. "Zustimmung und Kritik. Eine Bilanz." In *Einigung der Kirchen— reale Moglichkeit*, 157–89. Expanded 2d ed. Freiburg, 1985 (abbrev.: Fries).

Fries, Heinrich, and Karl Rahner. *Unity of the Churches: An Actual Possibility*. Translated by Ruth C. L. Gritsch and Eric W. Gritsch. Philadelphia: Fortress Press; New York and Ramsey, N.J.: Paulist Press, 1985 (German: *Einigung der Kirchen—reale Möglichkeit.* Freiburg, 1983) (abbrev.: Fries-Rahner).

Froehlich, Karlfried, ed. *Ökumene. Möglichkeiten und Grenzen heute. Zum 80. Geburtstag von O. Cullmann.* Tübingen: J. C. B. Mohr (Paul Siebeck), 1982 (abbrev.: *Möglichkeiten*).

————, ed. *Oscar Cullmann Vorträge und Aufsätze, 1925-1962.* Tübingen: J. C. B. Mohr (Paul Siebeck), 1966.

————, ed. *Testimonia oecumenica. Zum 80. Geburtstag von O. Cullmann.* Tübingen: Refo-Druck Hans Vogler, 1982 (abbrev.: *Test. oec.*).

Gagnebin, Laurent. "Compromis et ambiguités." *Etudes Théologiques et Religieuses* 58 (1983): 157-60.

Gherardini, Brunero. *Lutero-Maria. Pro o contra?* Pisa: Giardini, 1985.

Gounelle, André. "Inquiétudes et refus." *Etudes Théologiques et Religieuses* 58 (1983): 161-70.

Hammer, J., R. Ziegert, and A. Ahlbrecht. In *Ökumene am Ort. Blätter für ökumenische Basisarbeit* 8-9 (1985).

Hammann, Gottfried. *Entre la secte et la cité. Le projet d'Eglise du Réformateur Martin Bucer (1491-1551).* Geneva: Labor et Fides, 1984.

Hauck, Friedrich. "koinos. ktl." *Theological Dictionary of the New Testament,* edited by Gerhard Kittel, translated by Geoffrey Bromiley, 3:789-809. Grand Rapids: Wm. B. Eerdmans, 1965.

Hermesmann, Hans-Georg. *Zeit und Heil. Oscar Cullmanns Theologie der Heilsgeschichte.* Paderborn: Bonifacius-Druckerei, 1979.

Herms, Eilert. "Stellungnahme zum dritten Teil des Lima-Dokumentes 'Amt.'" *Kerygma und Dogma* 31 (1985): 65-96.

————. *Einheit der Christen in der Gemeinschaft der Kirchen. Die ökumenische Bewegung im Lichte der reformatorischen Theologie. Antwort auf den Rahnerplan.* Göttingen: Vandenhoeck & Ruprecht, 1984.

————. "Ökumene im Zeichen der Glaubenfreiheit." *Una Sancta* (1984): 193ff.

Joos, André. "Introduzione al Documento." In *Nicolaus. Rivista di Teologia ecumenico-patristica,* 193-228. Anno XI, fasc. 1. Bari: Istituto di Teologia ecumenico-patristica, 1983.

Jüngel, Eberhard. "Ein Schritt voran. Einigung der Kirchen als reale Möglichkeit." *Süddeutsche Zeitung* (Oct. 1-2, 1983).

Kallis, Anastasio. "Vorwort." *Artoklasis.* Münster, 1985.

Kasper, Walter. "Ökumenischer Fortschritt im Amtsverständnis?" In *Amt im Widerstreit,* edited by Karlheinz Schun, 52-58. Berlin: Morus, 1973.

————. "Das Petrusamt in ökumenischer Perspektive." In *In der Nachfolge Jesu Christi: Zum Besuch des Papstes,* edited by Karl Lehmann, 93-122. Freiburg, Basel, and Vienna: Herder, 1980.

————. "Zur Frage der Anerkennung der Ämter in der lutherischen Kirche." *Tübinger Quartalsschrift* 151 (1971): 97-109.

Küng, Hans. *On Being a Christian.* Translated by Edward Quinn. Garden City, N.Y.: Doubleday & Company, 1976.

Leenhardt, Fr. J. "Spiritualité catholique et spiritualité protestante, à-propos de Baptême—Eucharistie—Ministère." *Etudes Théologiques et Religieuses* 59 (1984).

Leuba, Jean-Louis. *Catholicité évangélique (Eglise et Liturgie)* 5 (Lausanne, Jan. 1985): 6ff.

_____. *Catholicité évangélique (Eglise et Liturgie)* 7 (Lausanne, July 1985): 45ff.

_____. *Institution et l'événement.* Neuchâtel: Delachaux & Niestlé, 1950.

_____. "Oecuménisme et confessions." *Internationale kirchliche Zeitschrift Z. 70 Geburtstag K. Stalders* (1987): 96ff.

Lienhard, Marc. *Martin Luther: un temp, une vie, un message.* Paris: Labor et Fides, 1983.

de Lubac, Henri. *Entretiens autour de Vatican II.* Paris, 1985.

Luther, Martin. *Lectures on Galatians 1535, Chapters 1-4.* LW, vol. 26. Translated and edited by Jaroslav Pelikan. St. Louis: Concordia Publishing House, 1963.

Maffei, G. *Il dialogo ecumenico sulla successione attorno all' opera di Oscar Cullmann.* Rome: Libreria Editrice Salesiana, 1979.

de Margerie, Bertrand. "L' analogie dans l'oecuménicité des Conciles notion clef pour l'avenir de l'oecuménisme." *Revue Thomiste* 84 (1984): 425–45.

Mehl, Roger. "Baptême, Eucharistie, Ministére." *Revue d'histoire et de philosophie religieuses* 63 (1983): 447–53.

Meyer, Harding. "The Decree on Ecumenism: A Protestant View." *Ecumenical Review* 37 (1985): 320–25.

_____. "Konsensus und Kirchengemeinschaft." *Kerygma und Dogma* 31 (1985): 174–200.

_____. *Luthertum und Katholizismus im Gespräch, Ergebnisse und Stand der katholisch-lutherischen Gespräche in den USA und auf Weltebene.* Frankfurt: Otto Lembeck, 1973 [The Malta Report].

Meyer, Harding, H. J. Urban, and Lukas Vischer, eds. *Documente wachsender Übereinstimmung Sämtliche Berichte und Konsenstexte interkonfessioneller Gespräche auf Weltebene 1931–1982.* Paderborn: Bonifacius-Druckerei; Frankfurt: Otto Lembeck, 1983.

"The Ministry in the Church, 1981." In *Growth in Agreement: Reports and Agreed Statements of Ecumenical Conversations at World Level*, edited by Harding Meyer, H. J. Urban, and Lukas Vischer, 248–75. Faith and Order Paper 108. New York: Paulist Press; Geneva: WCC, 1984 (German: "Das Geistliche Amt in der Kirche, 1981," in *Dokumente wachsender Übereinstimmung 1931–1982*, edited by Meyer, Urban, and Vischer, 329–57).

Nichols, Aidan. "One in Christ, Abbaye von Turvey." *L'Osservatore Romano* (Feb. 25–26, 1985).

Nissiotis, Nikos A. "Towards a New Ecumenical Era." *Ecumenical Review* 37 (1985): 321–35.

Ols, D. "Scorciatoie ecumeniche." *L'Osservatore Romano* (Feb. 25–26, 1985).

Ott, H. "Kann ein Petrusdienst in der Kirche einen Sinn haben?" *Concilium* (1975): 292ff.

Pannenberg, Wolfhart. "Die Arbeit von Faith and Order im Kontext der ökumenischen Bewegnung." *Ökumenische Rundschau* 31 (1982): 47ff.

————. "Die Bedeutung des Bekenntnisses von Nicaea-Konstantinopel für den ökumenischen Dialog." *Okumenische Rundschau* 31 (1982): 129–40.

————. "Einheit der Kirche als Glaubenswirklichkeit und als ökumenisches Ziel." *Una Sancta* 30 (1975): 220–21.

————. "Lima—pro und contra." *Kerygma und Dogma* 32 (1986): 35–51.

Plâmàdealâ, Antonie. "The BEM-Document in the Romanian Orthodox Theology: The Present Stage of the Discussions." *Romanian Orthodox Church News* (1985): 72–78.

Rahner, Karl. *Evangelisches Monatsblatt* (Bielefeld, 1982).

————. Interview in *Vie Protestante* (Lausanne, Feb. 1983).

Ratzinger, Joseph Cardinal. "Luther and the Unity of the Churches: An Interview with Cardinal Ratzinger." *Communio* 11 (1984): 210–26.

————. "Die ökumenische Situation—Orthodoxie, Katholizismus, Reformation." In *Theologische Prinzipienlehre. Bausteine zur Fundamentaltheologie*, 203–14. Munich: Erich Wewel, 1982.

————. *The Ratzinger Report: An Exclusive Interview on the State of the Church.* Interviewed by Vittorio Messori. Translated by Salvator Attanasio and Granan Harrison. San Francisco: Ignatius Press, 1985.

Ricca, Paolo. "Ende des Papsttums?" *Materialdienst der konfessionskundlichen Instituts Bensheim* 30 (1979): 106–11.

————. "Il BEM o il futuro dell'ecumenismo: Un parere sui documenti di Lima." *Protestantesimo* 38 (1983): 155–69, 225–43.

Sartori, Luigi. "Una risposta cattolica." In *Nicolaus. Rivista di Teologia ecumenico-patristica*, 229–58. Anno XI, fasc., 1. Bari: Istituto di Teologia ecumenico-patristica, 1983.

Schlink, Edmund. *Ökumenische Dogmatik. Grundzüge.* Göttingen: Vandenhoeck & Ruprecht, 1983.

Schutte, Heinz. *Amt. Ordination und Sukzession im Verständnis evangelischer und katholischer Exegeten und Dogmatiker der Gegenwart und in Dokumenten ökumenischer Gespräche.* Düsseldorf: Patmos, 1976.

Slenczka, Reinhard. "Die Konvergenzerklarungen zu Taufe, Eucharistie und Amt." *Kerygma und Dogma* 31 (1985): 2–19.

Stirnimann, Heinrich, and Lukas Vischer, eds. *Papsttum und Petrusdienst.* Frankfurt: Otto Lembeck, 1975.

Tappolet, Walter, and Albert Ebneter. *Das Marienlob der Reformatoren.* Tübingen: Katzmann, 1962.

Thurian, Max. *Kommentar zu den Lima-Erklärungen uber Taufe, Eucharistie und Amt.* Bensheimer Hefte 59. Göttingen: Vandenhoeck & Ruprecht, 1983.

————. "Una risposta protestante." In *Nicolaus. Rivista di Teologia ecumenico-patristica*, 271–84. Anno XI, fasc. 1. Bari: Istituto di Teologia ecumenico-patristica, 1983.

Tillard, J. M. *The Bishop of Rome*. Translated by John de Satgé. Wilmington, Del.: Michael Glazier, 1983.

Valeske, Ulrich. *Hierarchia veritatum. Theologischtliche Hintergrund und mögliche Konsequenzen eines Hinweises im Ökumenismusdekret des II. Vatikanischen Konzils zum zwischenkirchlichen Gesprach*. Munich: Claudius, 1968.

Vischer, Lukas. *Zusammenkunft des Zentralausschusses*. Canterbury; 1969.

──────. "After the Debate on Collegiality." *Ecumenical Review* 37 (1985): 306–19. (French: "L'accueil réservé aux débats sur la collégialité." In *La réception de Vatican II*, edited by Giuseppe Alberigo and Jean-Pierre Jossua, 305–25. Paris: Editions du Cerf, 1985.)

Visser't Hooft, W. A. *"The Development of Relations between the Ecumenical Movement and the Roman Catholic Church from 1914 to 1984"* (unpublished manuscript; last chapter edited later: "WCC–Roman Catholic Relations: Some Personal Reflections." *Ecumenical Review* 37 [1985]: 336–44).

Vögtle, Anton. "Jesus und die Kirche." In *Begegnung der Christen. Studien evangelischer und katholischer Theologen*. O. Karrer Festschrift, edited by Maximilian Poesle and Oscar Cullmann, 54–81. Stuttgart: Evangelisches Verlagswerk; Frankfurt: Josef Knecht–Carolusdruckerei, 1959.

──────. "Messiasbekenntnis und Petrusverheissung." *Biblische Zeitschrift* 1 (1957): 252–72; 2 (1958): 85–102.

Volk, Ernst. "Mahl des Herrn oder Mahl der Kirche?" *Kerygma und Dogma* 31 (1985): 33–64.

Willebrands, Johannes Cardinal. Press conference, Dec. 1985.

──────. "L'avenir de l'oecuménisme." *Proche Orient* (1975): 3–15.

──────. *Service d'Informations, Secrétariat pour l'Unité des chrétiens* 4 (1983): 133ff.